THE VANISHING HERO

THE VANISHING HERO

studies in novelists of the twenties

by

SEAN O'FAOLAIN

1956

EYRE & SPOTTISWOODE · LONDON

This book is printed in Great Britain for Eyre & Spottiswoode (Publishers) Ltd, 15 Bedford Street, London, W.C.2, by Jarrold and Sons Ltd, Norwich

Author's Note

In the Spring of 1953 I was invited to give six lectures at Princeton University as part of the Christian Gauss Seminars in Criticism. I have here expanded them into a book on the basis of further thought and the constructive comments of my listeners – or, as I prefer to think of them, my colleagues – during the, to me at least, valuable discussions that followed each lecture. I take this opportunity to express my warmest thanks to everybody who made my stay at Princeton such a pleasant three months; especially to the organisers of the Seminars and the Rockefeller Foundation who made my visit, those lectures and this book possible.

Contents

THE VANISHING HERO

THE FERVENT
TWENTIES

The novelists here dealt with were all, with the exception of Joyce, novelists of the Twenties. Virginia Woolf alone had published before 1920. Aldous Huxley's first novel appeared in that year; Miss Bowen's first stories in 1923; Waugh's first novel, *Decline and Fall* in 1928; Greene's *The Man Within* in 1929. The period attracted me for three reasons. I wanted to examine some of the basic assumptions of the novel in our time; I had formed an idea that the Twenties are a watershed or divide in the history of the contemporary novel; and it offered a group of writers with a large or completed body of work, some variety and evident distinction. The only reason why I did not go on to consider more novelists of the period was that I was confined to six lectures, and I thought it better to concentrate in each lecture on one writer. Originally I did not deal with Aldous Huxley at all, feeling that satire was sufficiently covered by Waugh, and suspecting what I have since decided is true, that Huxley is not properly speaking a satirist so much as a writer of brilliant invective.

I did not attempt to systematise the conclusions that presented themselves to me as I re-read these novelists. I feared to be tempted by the appeal of a schematical argument into forcing a theory instead of accumulating what I hoped would end up as an informative review of a literary period. But the theme did begin to force itself—that the central assumption of the contemporary novel, the one constant in all the writers before me, is the virtual disappearance from fiction of that focal character of the classical novel, the conceptual Hero. As so often happens the end of the journey now finds itself in the prospectus, these prefatory pages.

As I see the matter the Hero is a purely social creation. He represents, that is to say, a socially approved norm, for representing which to the satisfaction of society he is decorated with a title. The traditional novel had always moved about this socially acceptable character, so that even when he was not visibly or obtrusively present, as in *Les Liaisons Dangereuses* or *Manon Lescaut*, a form of lip-service was given to his hovering spirit by at least a final, formal admission that Crime Does Not Pay. The Hero was on the side of the long arm of the law, the *Sûreté*, the church, the kirk, the headmaster and the head of the family. He was on the side of Squire Allworthy, Mr John Knightley, Père Goriot, Mrs Proudie and Sherlock Holmes, or at least he was after he had been permitted a certain licence to roam in order to entertain us, and had duly returned to the bosom of conventional behaviour, as, for example, young Chuzzlewit returned, after "Eden" had reformed him, to the bosom of Mary Graham. Naturally some of the best novelists always kicked against this social convention, much to the satisfaction of the reading public and to the annoyance of the social critics; as happened to Scott when he wrote *Rob Roy* about a freebooter and Fielding when he wrote *Tom Jones* about a rascal. "A hero," cried Thackeray, of Tom Jones, somewhat hypocritically one fears, "with a flawed reputation, a hero sponging for a guinea, a hero who cannot pay his landlady, and is obliged to let his honour out to hire, is absurd, and the claim of Tom Jones to heroic rank is quite untenable." The reference to the landlady is the revealing item in the list. No man could be a hero if he was so anti-social as not to pay his debts.

The Hero, and his opposite number the Villain, represented in the traditional novel conflicts which they more or less clearly defined. That was in those good old days when novelists were prepared, with whatever mental reservations, to accept the fact that certain current ideas expressed firmly and clearly what the majority of people meant by a good or wholesome life. The novelist might not subscribe fully to these ideas or ideals himself; he might feel critical about them, poke fun at them, even reject them in his heart, but he could not deny that they formed the basis of the society in which he lived and which he described, and that anybody who rebelled against them, whether in real life or in fiction, must find himself not only in conflict with his community but in conflict with his origins and probably with his own nature. In admitting so much he admitted the concept of Heroism. If the novelist were a Stevenson, a Thackeray or a Dickens his readers knew where they were, and where the author stood, immediately they had identified the Hero. The identification was not always easy, especially with the French novelists. Many readers of the Abbé Prévost's entertaining account of the career of Manon Lescaut must have closed the book in a somewhat puzzled frame of mind as to the Abbé's convictions, in spite of his effort to clarify his position in the last few pages by bringing disaster on the head of his heroine. But one thing at least was clear about Manon, as about all other such strays from the narrow path: she was agin' the government, and she was therefore in a very proper danger of life and happiness. This would have soothed the Abbé's readers and increased their ambivalent pleasure in reading of her adventures. On the other hand, the first readers of de Laclos can have been in no doubt that his was a thoroughly subversive book. It is, perhaps, the first European novel without a hero; in other words it denies all social and moral values.

If, however, we will agree that most of our traditional certainties have become progressively less and less certain, it will be evident that the Hero as a personification of those certainties would also have to become less and less sure of his position. If I were to attempt to trace this gradual disintegration of the concept of the Hero in fiction I should have to write a separate book on the decline of morals in the nineteenth century. I am content to choose the one decade of the twentieth century which seems to illustrate the culmination of the process. But that this steady disintegration occurred becomes evident if we do no more than think of the difference between, say, Flaubert's Emma Bovary and Scott's Diana Vernon. If we agree that Diana is a "heroine" it is only by a violent extension of meaning that Emma can be also thought of as a "heroine". Here literature was anticipating life, in so far as Flaubert was dethroning the whole concept of the Hero by his mockery of those social values which alone guaranteed his validity. The Dreyfus case was to show clearly that the Hero was, in fact, a purely social concoction who could be enthroned and dethroned at will, be admired today, despised tomorrow and again admired the day after. In our own day Marshal Pétain was one of the saddest examples of this. The dictators were baser examples. Contemporary Russia has provided us with thousands of instances.

It will be prudent for me to observe here what I have already implied: that the concept of the Hero and the fact of the Brave Man are two different things, as I hope I make clear when dealing with the novels of Hemingway. I am not suggesting that bravery has disappeared from life or literature. What I do say is that the conceptual Hero has in our time been replaced by what, for want of a better word, we have come to call the anti-Hero. This personage is not a social creation. He is his own creation,

that is, the author's personal creation. He is a much less neat and
tidy concept, since he is always presented as groping, puzzled,
cross, mocking, frustrated and isolated, manfully or blunderingly
trying to establish his own personal, supra-social codes. He is
sometimes ridiculous through lack of perspicacity, accentuated
by a foolhardy if attractive personal courage. He is sometimes
intelligent, in the manner of Julien Sorel or Stephen Dedalus.
Whatever he is, weak or brave, brainy or bewildered, his one
abiding characteristic is that, like his author-creator, he is never
able to see any Pattern in life and rarely its Destination.

I have mentioned several novels from well behind our century
as a way of noting that this process has been going on for a long
time. If this reflects a general, slowly developing fissuration
in the main European tradition, which is to say the Christian
tradition, a social historian, like the literary historian, would need
to go back a very long way for its origins. Yeats thought that life
began to break into fragments between the death of Chaucer and
the birth of Shakespeare. Others might trace the disintegration
of traditional certainties to the decline of the aristocracy
in the seventeenth century; others might wish to begin with
the French Revolution; others blame Darwin; others Freud;
others the increase of scientific knowledge in our own generation
at such a rate that even scientific assurance has become loaded
with wonder and all matter has become liquefied by speculation.
Such considerations are beyond my province. All I can do is to
observe that if the handful of novelists I have chosen to consider
are representative of their period and of their vocation, most
men and women of literary talent who came to their majorities
around the year 1920 had begun thereabouts to think and to
write not as socially-integrated citizens but as more or less
isolated receptivities. Finding no satisfying sense of what I have
called Pattern or Destination in the social world they began,
in Aldous Huxley's image—it occurs in his Introduction to the

Letters of D. H. Lawrence, whom he sees as an example of the process–to dig out private caves, or air-raid shelters, of their own, and there they started to compose private satires, laments, fantasies and myths in the effort to fill the vacuum left by the death of the social Hero with a-social rebels, martyrs, misfits, minor prophets, or, in short, with aberrants and anti-Heroes. The chief function of these creations was to express the dissatisfaction of the young with the values of the old, and their fervent longing for a better pattern of living than they inherited, and for a more attractive destination than that to which their elders' pattern seemed likely to lead them.

They did not succeed in finding a better pattern. All they had was their fervour and their anger. Even the Catholics among them, that is, the few who should have been better equipped philosophically for practical living than their non-philosophically-minded friends, better equipped certainly than their positivist friends whose philosophy is entirely abstract and formalist–even these, Greene, Waugh, Scott-Fitzgerald, Hemingway, or their elders, such as Mauriac or Bernanos had no pattern of living that looked even in the least contemporary. Most of them were, rather, most exciting when, inspired by the Middle Ages, or earlier ages, they ignored the common human problem of living completely by submitting human beings to such a ruthless process of passionate intellectualisation that they have emerged in fiction not as autonomous men but as the galvanised puppets of their authors' transcendent ideas.

This fervour of the Twenties was not recognised at the time. Elderly gentlemen, as Mr Noel Annan has said of Leslie Stephen, cannot understand that "affectation, mockery, frivolity and extravagance are ways in which young men can criticise life seriously". The young were regarded by their elders as feckless and irresponsible. The authors they admired were considered as peculiar if interesting aberrants from the procession of

tradition–Remarque, Barbusse, Mrs Woolf, Eliot, Gertrude
Stein, Gide, Céline, Cocteau, the early Mann, the later Lawrence,
the later Joyce. In those days Bloomsbury was a joke-word, and
only journalists loved the apparently anarchist doings of the
fashionable or Bohemian young. And it must have been difficult
for anybody to realise that the real reason why young men
wanted to live with negresses, or develop tender homosexual
attachments, or conduct tense *ménages à trois*, or drink too
much, or be sexually promiscuous, or dig up Piccadilly at two
o'clock in the morning dressed in the costumes of Louis
XIV–there is a charming photograph of a group doing exactly
this in Patrick Balfour's reminiscences of the period, *Society
Racket*–was that they felt the urge of the most high-minded
ideals of personal sincerity and truthfulness to make some
gestures of defiance at the hypocrisies that had given them a
world unfit to live in. So far as I know it was not until the
nineteen-forties that criticism of the Twenties began to catch up
on prejudice. The first complete study of the period that I have
found–*Virginia Woolf and Bloomsbury*, by Irma Rantavaara–was
published in Helsinki in 1953. It is of interest that this study was
undertaken with the aid of a Rockefeller Grant; and that long
before that Virginia Woolf was respected, well-known and
carefully studied at the Sorbonne. The Twenties came into
their own in Britain as a serious and formative period rather
later than elsewhere.

I suppose it is fair to say that everybody now recognises that
it would be absurd to apply such terms as feckless or irresponsible
to a period that produced such writers as Mrs Woolf, Elizabeth
Bowen, Aldous Huxley, Graham Greene, Ernest Hemingway,
William Faulkner or Evelyn Waugh–the writers dealt with
in this book–all of whom are nowadays taken seriously, and
with one or two possible exceptions, better left unnamed,
considered quite respectable. And this is to make no mention

of writers whom even the period regarded as wholly traditional. Besides, to form a complete literary image of the time the generations must be allowed to overlap. D. H. Lawrence, John Cowper Powys, Joyce, Yeats, Lytton Strachey, Somerset Maugham were all writing at the top of their form in the Twenties. To leave these out because they were of an earlier generation would be to form a very squint-eyed picture of the decade. Furthermore, this overlapping of the generations is crucial for a reason apart altogether from literary figures; which is that tradition can sturdily persist behind all appearances of outward change. This is particularly true of Britain where influences can travel far and wide from sources unobserved at the time through a grape-vine network impossible to map until revealed slowly, and sometimes long after, by the publication of memoirs, letters, biographies or even State-papers. The Twenties have not in this respect been mapped at all so far.

Consider, to take but one example, the light thrown on the period by the short essay called "My Early Beliefs" by the late Lord Keynes. It appeared posthumously in 1949, in the little book called *Two Memoirs*. It was a paper written originally for a private club in 1938. Keynes was recording, for private ears, an influence that had a profound effect on his set as far back as 1903. I will come to the nature of this influence in a moment. Here let us first note how it spread, and continued into the Twenties. Note, first, the people who crop up in the memoir, all associates or old friends, sometimes referred to by Christian names or even pet-names—Bertie for Earl Russell, Ludwig for Ludwig Wittgenstein, Bob Trevy for the poet R. C. Trevelyan, Bunny for David Garnett, Clive for Clive Bell, and so on. Note then how they inter-connect. The first focus we observe is Cambridge. From Trinity College and King's: Bertrand Russell, R. C. Trevelyan, E. M. Forster, W. H. Macaulay, Desmond MacCarthy. (The one Oxford man is Lord Robert Cecil whose nephew Lord David Cecil was to marry MacCarthy's daughter.) We observe a familiar geographical and temperamental focus. Keynes was living at the time at 46 Gordon Square. Lady Ottoline Morrell, formerly Lady Bentinck, half-sister of the Duke of Portland, a great patroness, had married Philip Morrell and was living at 10 Gower Street. Clive Bell was living at 50 Gordon Square. He married Vanessa Stephen, the daughter of Leslie Stephen, and sister of Virginia Stephen who married Leonard Woolf. The Woolfs were living at 52 Tavistock Square, where they ran the Hogarth Press. This links up with the publishing business and, through Leonard, with the whole *Nation*, later *The New Statesman*, set, and many of the clever younger writers, such as Raymond Mortimer, Eddie Sackville-West, Stephen Spender, John Lehmann, Christopher Isherwood and William Plomer. When David Garnett joins forces with Francis Birrell to run a bookshop just behind Shaftesbury Avenue, we observe another link; with such publishers as Fisher Unwin and Jonathan Cape and another batch of young writers, through David's father Edward, one of the most influential publisher's readers of his time. We hear of others who foregathered in this set: Mark Gertler the painter, Roger Fry, Lytton Strachey, Goldsworthy Lowes Dickinson, Duncan Grant; several Cambridge dons, such as Sir Walter Durnford, Provost of King's College from 1918 to 1926; G. E. Moore, professor of philosophy, the McTaggart lecturer in moral sciences at Trinity from 1897 to 1923; and J. T. Sheppard, Provost of King's College after Durnford.

Now, if one were to trace the radiations from each of these through friends and professional connections one would evidently begin to get a widespreading map of unobtrusive but powerful influences in contemporary English thought. So, as one reads Virginia Woolf's *A Writer's Diary*, other names come in: Elizabeth Bowen, Rose Macaulay, Roger Senhouse,

whose name links us with another publishing house, that of
Secker and Warburg; Gerald Duckworth, another publisher,
who was half-brother to Virginia Woolf; Dorothy Wellesley
the poet, wife of Lord Gerald Wellesley, and later an intimate
friend of Yeats, Anthony Asquith.[1]

Now, of all these names, Lord Keynes was mainly concerned
in his memoir with one man and one book: the *Principia
Ethica* of G. E. Moore. Moore's book was published as far
back as 1903. Its influence was profound. "The habits of feeling,"
Keynes wrote of its influence, "formed then still persist in a
recognisable degree. It is those habits of feeling influencing the
majority of us which makes this Club a collectivity and separates
us from the rest. ... We never lost a resilience the younger
generation never seems to have had. They have enjoyed at
most only a pale reflection of something not altogether super-
seded, but faded and without illusions." (This "faded and
without illusions" may suggest at once both his own inadequacy
to pass on a message of great value and the cooler mood of the
Thirties listening with respect but with less hope to their elders.)
But when we see what was taught by this "Sacred Book" of
Moore's, as it has been called by Mr Noel Annan, we see that
something of its message must nevertheless have seeped through.

It may be that the still popular phrase "state of mind" ("My
dear, I found him in *such* a state of mind!") originated with
Moore. For the core of the Moore position was that (quoting
Keynes) "nothing mattered except states of mind ... not
associated with action or achievement. ... They consisted in
timeless, passionate states of contemplation and communion,
largely unattached to 'before' and 'after'." I think anybody
reading the novels of the Twenties might well have occasion

---

[1] I am here much indebted to a Third Programme Talk by Mr Noel Annan
on "The Mood of the Twenties", printed in *The Listener*, February 8th, 1951.
Mr Annan's biography of Leslie Stephen is also suggestive. On Mrs Woolf's
death appreciations in *Horizon* intimately evoked the original Bloomsbury.

to revert constantly to these two things: the divorce from *achievement*; and the consequential detachment *in time* from "before" and "after". (It would be amusing to think that we could link up, say, Graham Greene's or Ernest Hemingway's concept of time as "screened at both ends" with the *Principia Ethica* of Cambridge rationalism.) The appropriate subjects of contemplation, while in these timeless states of mind, were a beloved person, beauty and truth; and the prime objects in life were held to be Love, "the creation and enjoyment of aesthetic experience and the pursuit of knowledge". It was not, however, a hedonist philosophy. It was an Epicurean philosophy. Its disciples thought themselves rationalists to begin with, dis-covered only when they had been involved that they were Neoplatonists, and were ultimately to confess, as Keynes did, that their religion within this philosophy closely followed the English Puritan tradition of being chiefly concerned with the salvation of their own souls. Pleasure was sternly decried, though, as the world drew them out, it had to be admitted that the Neoplatonic contemplation of physical female beauty did tend to the carnal enjoyment thereof, and that as the first rapture wore away there entered into the lives of the disciples of idealism what the language of the period described as hot intrigues. But, at first, they were so serious about everything that when Keynes and Sheppard maintained one night that there was nothing wrong in itself about being cheerful they at once fell into deep disgrace in their set.

Now, the cardinal point in all this is the reference to personal salvation. For, essentially this ethic of Moore's is a thorough-going defence of individualism, and as such must have entirely pleased the individualistic Twenties. If, however, we see that the effect was to draw people away from the older, Victorian social-minded ethic, which saw man as a servant of his society, as undoubtedly happened, this was not entirely Moore's fault.

It is true that Moore argues that it is a logical error to suppose
that the good can be defined as whatever gives the greatest
happiness to the greatest number; that the good is distinct, to
be appreciated by personal intuition, enjoyed and contemplated
when one is in a good state of mind; but he did consider rules
of conduct. However:

"We set on one side [Keynes records] not only that part of
Moore's fifth chapter on 'Ethics in relation to Conduct' which dealt
with the obligations so to act as to produce by causal connection the
most probable maximum of eventual good through the whole
procession of future ages, but also that part which described the duty
of the individual to obey general rules. We entirely repudiated a
personal liability on us to obey general rules. We claimed the right
to judge every individual case on its merits, and the wisdom, experience and self-control to do so successfully. This was a very important
part of our faith and for the outer world our most important and
dangerous characteristic. We repudiated entirely customary morals,
traditions and traditional wisdom. We were, that is to say, in the
strict sense of the term immoralists."

The stress, then, is on personal sincerity. Its source lies in the
optimism of the first decade of the century, "the undisturbed
individualism of those Edwardian days". When the second
decade was broken by the war of 1914, and the third decade
was darkened by the disillusion of 1918 and after, the need for
personal sincerity became not less but more urgent. It was to
become the hallmark of the decade of disillusion never again
to hope except in total honesty.

The irony of it was that the sincerity of those Epicurean
forerunners did not, in fact, appeal at all, in the form of its
original definition, to the young people who came of age in
the Twenties. It was too withdrawn, too hothouse, perhaps
they would have said it was smug. Even Keynes had come to see
that there was some truth in this attitude, as he admits in his

last paragraph referring to a writer who was very close to the heart of the Twenties, D. H. Lawrence:

"And if I imagine us as coming under the observation of Lawrence's ignorant, jealous, irritable, hostile eyes, what a combination of qualities we offered to arouse his passionate distaste: this thin rationalism skipping on the crust of the lava, ignoring both the reality and the value of the vulgar passions, joined to libertinism and comprehensive irreverence . . . a regular skin-poison. All this was very unfair to poor, silly, well-meaning us. But . . . there may have been just a grain of truth when Lawrence said, in 1914, that we were 'done for'."

The ungrateful young people of the Twenties were to agree in general with Lawrence's "done for"; and in agreeing they were to lump all their elders together, indiscriminately. It is only now, when they are themselves in their fifties, that they are able to discriminate calmly between elders and elders, and to realise how far some of these elders were their creditors. The reason they did not see and acknowledge it earlier is that there was a split in their ranks around the early Thirties when the Pylon Poets appeared, hailing the coming, social revolution, finding their inspiration in machinery and the masses, basing their attitude to life on the need for being thoroughly social-minded. Then came the Spanish Civil War, and then the Second World War, when for a period Russia was the darling of the social-minded Left. The Socialist triumph in Britain after the war and the utter cynicism of the Russians' political technique shook these apples off every tree. Before 1950 there was already hardly a writer left in Britain who any longer thought it essential to be social-minded. Moreover, there had been such a hullabuloo of admiration for "the people" during the war that everybody became sick to death of them. The upshot of it all is that the term "anti-social" no longer now has the awful meaning of a selfish insistence on individual liberty harmful to society. If anything "anti-social" means the opposite—a selfish insistence

by the greedy masses on their rights, harmful to individual
liberty. Mr Noel Annan has drawn attention to the fact that
this is the wheel coming full circle; for, away back in the
Epicurean hey-day, this was precisely how "anti-social" was
defined by Bertrand Russell: as the equation of anti-individualist.
It was the natural Epicurean attitude, and it was the natural
attitude of all the young people after the First World War.

From what other attitude could have come all those (so often
boring and whining) novels about young men with obtuse
fathers, young men who had been bullied at school, young men
hopelessly misunderstood in dull bourgeois homes? Indeed, it
was then that the word bourgeois first began to take on a
pejorative sense, but for reasons of sensibility and not for political
reasons. The Pylon Poets twisted it to their own uses, never
thinking what types had first dethroned it. The word has, alas,
never been rehabilitated. There was a snobbery about poverty
after the Twenties. Men like Sean O'Casey became lords of
poverty, and men like Mr John Betjeman had to arrive before
anybody born with even an electro-plated spoon in his mouth
ceased to cringe at the charge of having been born of respectable
or well-off parents. But the bourgeois virtues, and they are
many, have not appealed to writers since then. Mr Waugh,
born of that sound stock, sold his inheritance for the aristocracy,
the Catholic Church and the British Army. His contemporaries
sold their inheritance for nothing at all.

Not, to be sure, that Bloomsbury was the whole of the
Twenties, even of the literary Twenties. It had no direct
influence, for example, on Waugh, though I find it hard to
believe that he could have been entirely unaware of it. (Was
anybody at the time entirely unaware of it?) He would, at
least, without knowing very much about it—he admits that he
never heard of G. E. Moore—have scorned it, been one of those
who thought it too hothouse, too withdrawn, too afraid of the

wide world. One reason why he would not have been influenced, at least through personal contact, by the sort of people Keynes mentions is that he was not a Cambridge man. Of the Bloomsbury set (so far as I know) only Raymond Mortimer and Cyril Connolly did not come from the younger university, and Connolly was never trusted by Bloomsbury. This is the significance of the reference in Mrs Woolf's *Diary* to "those trusty Cambridge chaps". Unlike "the Grigs" (meaning Mr Geoffrey Grigson) they could always be expected to sympathise with her work. Indeed, they encouraged her loyally and effectively, if also, far too uncritically. Waugh belonged to a much gayer set, a sort of High Bohemia centred around Lady Cunard, Lord Berners and the Sitwells, a blend of the more eccentric aristocracy and the more amusing artists who destroyed the old-fashioned Low Bohemia of Augustus John. The sort of people who visited Lord Berners at Farringdon were certainly very different from the intellectuals who drank cocoa and talked late into the night at Gordon Square. They included such people as all "the Mitford girls", "the Lygon girls" (Lord Beauchamp's daughters), John Betjeman, Lady (Dolly) Castlerosse, Phyllis de Janzé–she ran a fashionable hatshop in Bond Street–Lettice ("Duchess") Ashley-Cooper, Patrick Balfour. Of Lord Berners one is told that, not caring for the colour-scheme of his fields, he had his cows painted blue. Apocryphal or not, the story suggests that although he also had a town house, where the Oxford-Cambridge paths must sometimes have crossed, one cannot make too much of the fact. The two sets could also have crossed paths at Rosa Lewis's pub in Jermyn Street after the races, and it is unlikely that any of the guests spent much time there discussing the true, the beautiful and the good. Nevertheless, though the gay and the serious may not have mingled frequently or intimately, and though the Mitford Girls, or the Lygon Girls, or Mr Waugh may not have spent much of their wild youth in reading, they must occasionally have read something. By the time Waugh was writing his first book Mrs Woolf had published nine books; Eliot four; and E. M. Forster had completed his canon. It is inconceivable that such books were not known to High Bohemia. However, I have no wish to suggest to any living relict of High Bohemia that he or she sometimes stole away quietly from the champagne-bucket to the cocoa-samovar to practise high thinking in secret in a Bloomsbury flatlet. All one may fairly stress is that when we read the novels of Waugh, or even of Miss Mitford, as when we read the poetry of John Betjeman, we must often not only feel the old *accedia*, the old sadness, the old seriousness breaking through the superficial light-heartedness but feel that it is this undertone which gives to their work whatever lasting value time will accord to it.

They were all sad young men, but they had great courage; after all, they looked coldly enough at life, and then had the courage to handle its unattractive, apparently unmalleable material, to create, to give birth in days of famine. They may have been a generation astray but they were not in the least a lost generation. They made literature out of loss—Huxley has been doing it all his life; so did Scott-Fitzgerald. They wrote and composed under a sense of doom, beating time. It is the feeling one always gets from Gershwin's *Rhapsody in Blue* : that opening, sky-rocketing, dismayed wail of the clarinet, the frightening, mocking meouwings of the saxophone, the hurrying speed as of men hurrying to get their song finished before the train crashes, the pianist dropping nervously the premonitory rains of the coming thunderstorm, the famous central melancholy melody that might well be the decade's Hymn to Sorrow, its elegy for The Good Time Our Fathers Lost Us. Sad, yes, but only because they wanted so much that life should be worthy of itself, laughing even as they thought of it with twisted mouths,

suffused by a desperate frenzy to unfurl a flag. It was equally in
keeping that Waugh should have become a Commando in the
Second World War, and that Huxley should have retired to the
desert and mysticism, a marooned pirate throwing out endless
bottles of invective from his sandy shore. It was anything but a
disheartening period. A period that laid the greatest possible
strain on the individual soul produced some of the strongest
personal assertions in our time. If affirmations were beyond them
that was not their fault. Nobody can affirm out of personal integrity alone. Only when certainty returns to men at large, that
is to what we call the world, can affirmation return to literature,
and with it the representative Hero. And that, surely depends on
the re-emergence for the purposes of the arts of a general body
of human faith? (A large subject on which I have inadequately
touched in my final essay.) Nobody wants affirmation for
affirmation's sake. It depends on what is affirmed. As well as
Barbarossa there are the barbarians. Sometime in the Twenties
a cartoon in *Simplicissimus* mentioned this dilemma by depicting
Barbarossa leaning asleep over his table, his beard growing
down through the slab, while on the ground beneath, also
awaiting in his sleep the trumpet-call of the resurrection, lay
Kaiser Wilhelm, his pointed moustaches horning up through
the heroes' table. It is an inelegant problem on which even
now, perhaps more than ever now, it is impossible to make
any elegant comment. Since we became aware of it we have
all been stumbling. One recurs to the thought that the wonder
of the Twenties was not so much that they wrote so well but
that they wrote at all. Perhaps their secret recipe was to make
themselves our scapegoats. The novelist, unable to establish
any happy equilibrium between his personality and his milieu,
sacrificed himself and his characters, the two imaginatively
one, for our sake. Whether a Christian or not, he relived the
Christian myth, with the vast difference that his martyrdom was

entirely gratuitous in that he redeemed nobody but himself.
It seems a better way of seeing modern literature than when
Mlle Claude-Edmonde Magny suggests that Faulkner exorcises
his agony by brushing it off on the reader. The truth seems to
be, rather, that Faulkner dies in agony all over again every time
he writes a novel. Or perhaps Camus is more to the essential
point when he says, in *L'Homme Revolté*, that "the individualist
cannot accept history as it is: he must destroy reality, not
collaborate with it, in order to affirm his own existence".
Which implies an utter revolt that has forced the conceptual
Hero to give way to a new central type, whether Spartacus
or Sebastian, the tortured Martyr.

HUXLEY and WAUGH

or

I do not think, therefore I am

One of the more fascinating and tantalising problems that face the reader of fiction is to see how, and how far, a novelist can or does convey his own attitude to life through characters for whose views it would be impertinent to hold him responsible, and for whose behaviour he can, at most, be held only partly responsible. It is a major problem for the reader of the novels of Aldous Huxley since so many of his characters are continually uttering opinions on all sorts of subjects, and since so many of them are so unattractive that the general picture of the life they lead is, though described with wit and intelligence, more than depressing. Do these novels surreptitiously reflect Mr Huxley's view of life at the time he wrote them, or was he an entirely neutral reporter dissociating himself utterly from what he reported? Are those novels faithful documentaries? Or are they personal parables?

Since I not only read them as entertaining personal parables but regard all novels, other than novels of pure pastime, as entertaining personal parables, it will be well for me to define a novel forthwith. A novel is a narrative, dealing with a number of characters whom the author has succeeded in making interesting and persuasive, and whom he deploys in a manner which, with his personal view of life, he considers fitting, and we with him. The fate, the views, the passions, the follies, the prejudices which he bestows on his characters imply his unspoken comment on life in general. For he does not need at any time to give explicit utterance to any comment; he will hope rather to elicit some comment from the reader; and if he elicits from us what he considers the correct comment he has succeeded in writing a persuasive novel. He has also, so to speak, given himself away, since our comment is his, inserted into our minds by suggestion under the hypnosis of the dramatic spectacle he has invented. Even his selection of certain types, out of all possible types, must be taken as intimating some such intention on his part; and when, as Huxley did in those novels of the Twenties, he repeats himself in this way he must be emphasising his intention. It is for us to free ourselves from his hypnotic suggestion, to open our minds to the pattern he is emphasising, to consider it by the light of our own experience, or imaginative sympathy, to agree with its relevance to actual life or to disagree with it. This is why, incidentally and relevantly, there is, properly speaking, no such thing as historical fiction, since history lays obvious limitations on a writer's personal choice of types and above all on his autonomy in deploying them towards what he, with his view of life, considers their fitting behaviour and fate. What I am saying is really an old thing: that every creative writer is to a large degree writing himself and that there is, ultimately, no such state of mind for a creative writer as total detachment.

Huxley has always shown a good deal of skill in giving us the illusion that he is quite detached or neutral. It is, however, almost entirely the illusion of one form of detachment, that which the intelligent writer may achieve–or seem to achieve– by the practice of intellectual discipline. Unfortunately for himself as a novelist he has practically nothing of that power– which Joyce, for instance, possessed in abundance, and which is essential to the truly effective novelist—whereby a writer associates himself sympathetically (or if one prefers empathically) with his characters in all their feelings, while skilfully concealing the fact from us. His intellect works too hard for that. His human sympathy is limited. His persuasiveness is of the order of a witty radio-commentator announcing plausibly, "Now Gumbril is saying ... Mrs Aldwinkle is now entering the room ... Mr Quarles thinks that ..." We concentrate on the momentary saying, doing and thinking; the characters in their roundness—not that they have any roundness—easily disappear from our minds; we really scarcely see them at all; it is like a film in which only the sound-track is working and the screen is blank; we are conscious only of the skill of the script-writer. At that point the illusion of intellectual detachment breaks down since we realise that the whole comedy has been manipulated by the author for his own purposes. With a true novelist, actually detached or not, we believe that the characters are autonomously alive and by this livingness they make us forget the author. The result is that when we recall the novels of Mr Huxley we never talk much about the characters but a great deal about Mr Huxley and his ideas.

This does not mean, however, that the ideas of his characters are his ideas. For example:

"They sat a long time over their cigarettes; it was half past three before Mrs Viveash suggested they should go.

"'Almost time,' she said, looking at her watch, 'to have tea. One damned meal after another. And never anything new to eat. And every year one gets bored with another of the old things. Lobster, for instance, how I used to adore lobster once! But today—well, really, it was only your conversation, Theodore, that made it tolerable.'

"Gumbril put his hand to his heart and bowed. He felt suddenly extremely depressed.

"'And wine: I used to think Orvieto so heavenly. But this spring, when I was in Italy, it was just a bad muddy sort of Vouvray. And

those soft caramels they call Fiats; I used to eat those till I was sick.
I was at the sick stage before I'd finished one of them, this time in
Rome.' Mrs Viveash shook her head. 'Disillusion after disillusion.'"

Huxley does not here say that life is disillusion after disillusion.
It is Mrs Viveash who says it. Nevertheless, the general tone
and effect of the passage is so often repeated in those first four
novels that we become sensitive to the emphasis and seek for
the purpose of it. When this theme of the disillusioning effect
of a surfeit of pleasure recurs and recurs, when so many characters are made to chase pleasure and find it so often dust and
ashes, we are driven to think that Huxley is, in effect, saying
that for such people as he so frequently depicts all pleasure,
and it may be all happiness, is an illusion. The question straight-
way arises in our minds: are these types abnormal, does he
consider them abnormal and are we expected to think of them
as abnormal? It would appear from the epigraph which he
selected for *Point Counterpoint* that he considers them types of
all humanity:

> *Oh, wearisome condition of humanity,*
> *Born under one law, to another bound,*
> *Vainly begot and yet forbidden vanity,*
> *Created sick, commanded to be sound.*
> *What meaneth nature by these diverse laws,*
> *Passion and reason, self-division's cause?*

Abnormal they may be to us; they are to him parables of the
normal problem of mankind, though not necessarily of mankind's normal handling of the diverse laws of nature. This
parabolic treatment permits Huxley to present us with a set of
somewhat fantastic characters, even eccentrics, and extravagant
situations without arousing our protest or disbelief–disbelief
never even arises, nor belief either: such as the baron or the
scientist in *After Many a Summer* and the whole idea of recessive
rejuvenation. It is not the characters we are intended to accept,

or not more than is necessary to sustain a mild interest and qualified assent; it is the moral to which their behaviour points, and some—it is impossible to say which—of the ideas they propound.

For the multitude of brilliant and amusing ideas in which these novels abound cannot be ignored as part, even though what part nobody can say, of the general parable. Indeed, the trouble with them is that they tend to swamp the novels as novels, a fact which Huxley was probably admitting through the Notebook of Philip Quarles in *Point Counterpoint*, in such passages as:

"Novel of ideas. The character of each person must be implied, as far as possible, in the ideas of which he is the mouthpiece. In so far as theories are rationalisations of sentiments, instincts, dispositions of soul, this is feasible. The chief defect of the novel of ideas is that you must write about people who have ideas to express—which excludes all but about ·01 of the human race. Hence the real, the congenital novelists don't write such books. But then I never pretended to be a congenital novelist."

And again:

"The great defect of the novel of ideas is that it's a made-up affair. Necessarily; for people who can reel off neatly-formulated notions aren't quite real; they're slightly monstrous. Living with monsters becomes tiresome in the long run."

These, then, are novels of ideas which are the rationalisations (to use Philip Quarles's words) of certain sentiments, instincts, dispositions of soul in a number of characters selected to convey the author's life-view and to point his moral.

I use the word moral uncomfortably. It is too explicit to indicate the general impression with which we are left. Yet some such word seems necessary to indicate that Huxley gives us throughout the strongest feeling that he has been trying to leave us with more than a vague, general impression. The

critical quality of his approach, the highly intelligent mind
that he displays, the ostensibly neutral or detached attitude of
the stratospheric intellectual surveying the follies of mankind
seem to promise a general conclusion, or set of conclusions,
which is a much more pointed thing than a general impression.
The "congenital" novelist is content with drawing a wash of
feeling, like a wash of colour, over the landscape of life; he
communicates his instinctive feelings rather than his logical
certainties. One, rightly or wrongly, expects more, being led
to expect more, from the novelist of ideas. But the deeper source
of my discomfort in using the word *moral* in this context is the
sense of disappointed expectation that attaches to it, and which,
if valid generally–if, that is, it is not merely a personal expectation which others do not also feel–points to Huxley's central
problem and weakness as a novelist. For the general conclusion,
or moral, or practical lesson, or general principle of the author's
thought or life-view does not in the end emerge with anything
like the clarity one expects from a man of such apparently
superlative intelligence. All one can do is to induce it confusedly
and unsatisfactorily from the underlying spirit of invective,
which one feels to be just as instinctive and emotional as in any
congenital novelist. One is finally driven to conclude that all
Huxley's intellectual paraphernalia conceals an intelligence at
war with itself, or struggling vainly for a clear position from
which to attack. And while in this essay I am interested directly
only in the early novels, it would be unrealistic not to bear in
mind, also, the constant gropings and changes of position in his
later work.

The result has been that he has from the beginning attempted
satire and achieved only what I have called invective. The
absence of a firm standpoint made this inevitable, since of its
nature satire implies a clear standpoint, or acceptable norm,
from which to castigate those who would deny, insult or attempt

to overthrow it. Breughel's pictures of country boors at play are in this sense aristocratic pictures, and imply not his judgements alone but those of his society. Pope's satires are the judgements of a devoted, even fanatical Tory driven to despair of his country by the triumph of the Whigs. That the standpoint of either may be absurd or perverse does not arise, except in final judgements of the universality and permanence of their ideas, whereupon one may elevate Boileau or Pascal above Pope or Breughel. If satire were not firmly based in this way on some widely accepted norm it might well be considered an impertinence on the part of any man to put himself into the judgement seat; wherefore it has been well said of Pope, by Mark Pattison, that it was well for him that his personal spite, pettiness, meanness, ungenerosity and vanities were balanced by his debt to the universal spirit of his age. It was Huxley's misfortune as a would-be satirist to have been born into an age in which the writer found himself a rebel against all tradition. His great interest for us, as it must be for subsequent generations, lies in his being such a perfect representative of an angry and disoriented decade gallantly exploring a sea of doubt; though it would be unjust and incomplete to regard him merely as the castigator of one peculiar, or abnormal, set of people: these are the means, or metaphors, by which he expresses the perplexities inherited by his decade as a whole from what it considered its unworthy ancestry.

What a living image he presents to us of that era, at once bored and perplexed, disillusioned and unhappy, bewildered and groping, lost and seeking for firm land, now excited, now hopeful, now overcome by despair! He conveys it for the most part by juxtaposition, by point and counterpoint. So, in *Those Barren Leaves*:

"'I don't see that it would be possible to live in a more exciting age,' said Calamy. 'The sense that everything's perfectly provisional and temporary – everything, from social institutions to what we've hitherto regarded as the most sacred scientific truths – the feeling that nothing, from the Treaty of Versailles to the rationally explicable universe, is really safe, the intimate conviction that anything may happen, anything may be discovered – another war, the artificial creation of life, the proof of continued existence after death – why it is all infinitely exhilarating.'

"'And the possibility that everything may be destroyed?' questioned Mr Cardan.

"'That's exhilarating too,' Calamy answered, smiling.

"'It may be rather tame of me,' Mr Cardan said, 'but I confess, I prefer a more quiet life. I persist that you made a mistake in so timing your entry into the world that the period of your youth coincided with the war and your early maturity with this horribly insecure and unprosperous peace ...'"

And he proceeds to contrast his own youth, spent in calm faith in the placid bosom of nineteenth-century materialism. It is a characteristic contrast between Calamy, the sincere if weak romantic who will end up as a sort of mystic, and Cardan, the self-avowed practical man and almost total sceptic who impresses himself as something of a sponger. A few pages on the counterpoint is repeated on the terrace of Mrs Aldwinkle's house when that lady, who has believed too long "in passion, passionately", feels that the starry nights of Italy explain the passion of the South, and Calamy agrees, but Cardan twists it all around to the climate, the effect of heat on inducing idleness, the ample leisure that accompanies idleness and the evident conclusion that: "Passion can only flourish among the well-fed unemployed." It is a typical Huxleyan sequence, written in a technique of non-committal irony which is much more near to the irresponsibility of Restoration comedy than the didactic comedy of Shaw. The ideas are adumbrated with a sceptical smile – and left unresolved. Yet they *are* adumbrated, in the form either of difficult, if not unanswerable, questions or of opposing theories, sometimes explicitly stated by their own type-characters but not always stated, sometimes merely indicated by their behaviour, their dilemmas, the predicaments into which they get themselves by having been all too true to type.

Those Barren Leaves is one of the most readable, representative, effective and clear of Huxley's novels. It will show us more easily than any other of his novels how he proceeds. The novel is placed chiefly in Italy, with flash-backs to England. Somewhere in the Apuan hills, near Spezia, a sagging huntress of social and literary lions named Lilian Aldwinkle has bought a Malaspina palace, wherein she collects a number of guests. The device is a simple one–a cruising liner, an island, an inn cut off by the snow, a long-distance bus; they have often been used for this purpose by novelists who either want dramatic action or psychological analysis. Huxley is not interested in either; he chiefly wants to set his people talking; he does stoop to a few elementary events or episodes but, as in the Aristotelian *Poetics*, these are not much more than a break or rift in the choric songs which give us the main continuity. The main characters, besides Mrs Aldwinkle herself, are her pretty niece Irene; Miss Thriplow, a Chelsea-ish novelist; a self-indulgent, fruity, obscurely gifted professional week-ender named Cardan; Mr Falx, a Labour leader; Lord Hovenden, immensely rich, a Guild Socialist, under the influence of Falx; and Calamy, an intelligent, serious-minded bachelor who shares the role of central character with one Francis Chelifer, a cynical, self-disbelieving dilettante who composes occasional poems and witty aphorisms when not editing, in Gog's Court, Fetter Lane, *The Rabbit Fancier's Gazette* with which is incorporated *The Mouse Breeder's Record*. He is not well-off; he lives in a Chelsea boarding-house. Mrs Aldwinkle literally picked him up off the beach after he had been all but drowned. His mother, Mrs Chelifer, also appears, and a dotty creature named Miss Elver whose brother has brought her to Italy in the feeble-minded hope that she will die of malaria and that he will inherit her fortune.

It emerges that Miss Thriplow is a self-conscious woman who has so corroded her natural emotions by constantly dramatising them that it would not be unjust to describe her as almost completely bogus. That the serious-minded Calamy should casually bed with her is clearly intended not as a tribute to her charms but to the frailty of his intelligence and his will, and since he ultimately retires to a peasant's hut to ponder upon the inmost nature of reality, we cannot help feeling that we are intended to look back with grave apprehensions from the hardships of a peasant's pallet to the pleasures of a lady's bed. Cardan emerges as a pragmatist, a materialist, a self-called practical man, and we must conclude that we are to trace his boasted realism to a core of weak self-indulgence when we see him marrying the unfortunate lunatic, Miss Elver, for her money. Mrs Aldwinkle decides that Chelifer is a Shelley barely saved from drowning, and in her foolish romanticism she shamelessly tries to make him her lover. She is represented pitilessly as an ageing Juno chasing impossible young love. We discover in Chelifer a thoroughly disillusioned cynic. In this atmosphere Falx might well fear that the young girl Irene must end by being corrupted—he thinks of the palace as "a bad house"—but Hovenden happily falls in love with her and, we may believe, saves her from destruction. It is without regret that we note that Hovenden and Irene have no clever ideas to propound: indeed, the only occasion when Irene does propound a "clever" idea—that "contraception has made chastity superfluous"—is that on which Falx begins to foresee her ruin. But, then, they are both simple souls, somewhat reminiscent of Nina and Adam in *Vile Bodies*, and Huxley is not, one feels, greatly interested in simple souls.

Nor, to be honest, are we in this novel. Our interest is in the play of opposing ideas. Of these ideas the clearest exponents are Francis Chelifer, Calamy and Cardan. They represent three concepts of reality. To Chelifer reality is what it seems to ninety-nine out of every hundred human beings, and he maintains that nobody has any right to run away from those brutish minds who preponderate in the universe. Calamy disagrees. Such people, in his view as a seeker after ulterior reality are "content with appearances", such as the Harrow Road and the Café de la Rotonde, "call them realities and proceed to abuse any one who takes an interest in what lies underneath these superficial symbols as a romantic imbecile". Reality, to Cardan, is the social system where the wise man steers his way cunningly between the tribalistic Babbitts, over whom Chelifer gloats masochistically, and the few hyper-optimists like Calamy who shelter from the more unpleasant aspects of human behaviour by simply dismissing them as surface appearances. If we could fully respect any of these three men, or feel that any of them had made, or was likely to make, an honourable success of his life we might feel that Huxley was using them to lead us to his own general conclusion. As it is we are presented with three ways of life none of which, evidently, persuades him, and we must feel that the mockery he turns on all three characters reflects his despair at the power of human intelligence, including his own, to answer the problem he poses. At this point in our reading we might begin to be doubly glad that the only two people, Hovenden and Irene, who come out of the novel with some hope of happiness have no intellectual views on the subject at all. Had they been permitted any, they too, one fears, would have also been eviscerated by the invective of Huxley's pervasive misanthropy.

But every novel contains at least one character who seems closer to the sympathies of the author than any other, and one is aware of an increase of heat and interest whenever he takes the stage. Here the temperature of our interest rises whenever Chelifer appears. Certainly the section called "Fragments from the Autobiography of Francis Chelifer" has more life in it than any other, especially Chapter Five, wherein Huxley has embedded an excellent short story beginning: "Her name was Barbara Waters." Here, at least, the moral is quite clear. Indeed, it is stated with passion.

Through Barbara, we are told, Chelifer learned the difficult art of "exclusive concentration on the relevant", meaning "the human reality in the centre of the pointless landscape". Barbara was more than his charmer; she was his symbol of "an intense and secret and utterable happiness". She had haunted him by her mysterious beauty when a boy; he meets her again during the war and is enraptured again to find that "within its ambush her soul kept incessant holiday". He continues to idealise her; but, now, he who had "desired all beauty, all that exists of goodness and truth, symbolised and incarnate in one face", begins to desire her as an individual woman, and he both nourishes this natural desire and fears the revelation of its satisfaction. One foresees the result.

"All this [he writes, in his Autobiography, looking back sadly at it] were it to happen to me now would seem perfectly natural and normal. If I were to make love to a young woman I should know precisely what I was making love to. But that, in those days, was something I had still to learn. In Barbara's company I was learning it with a vengeance. I was learning that it is possible to be profoundly and slavishly in love with some one for whom one has no esteem, whom one does not like, whom one regards as a bad character and who, finally, not only makes one unhappy but bores one. And why not, I might now ask, why not? That things should be like this is probably the most natural thing in the world. But in those days I imagined that love ought always to be mixed up with affection and admiration, with worship and an intellectual rapture, as unflagging as that one experiences during the playing of a symphony. Sometimes, no doubt, love does get involved with some or all of those things; sometimes these things exist by themselves, apart from love. But one must be prepared to swallow one's love completely neat and unadulterated. It is a fiery, crude and somewhat poisonous draught."

It is a summary of what happens to almost every character in Huxley's novels who "tries" love. It is an echo of Mrs Viveash's "disillusion after disillusion". Barbara's mysterious, unearthly beauty is the mask of a trollop in a state of almost constant heat. Because he has idealised her he suffers agonies of unhappiness at the loss of his dream. "I was happy at the thought that I should soon be kissing her; miserable because that was not how I wanted to love my imaginary Barbara; miserable too, when I secretly admitted to myself the existence of the real Barbara, because I felt it an indignity to be the slave of such a mistress." One thinks of Tony Last in Waugh's *A Handful of Dust*: "A whole Gothic world had come to grief..." when Chelifer says: "Reality gave imagination the lie direct."

When all self-deception ends, he adds up the sum of his tormenting experience and the answer is:

"And it is the truth that men are cruel and stupid and that they suffer themselves to be driven to destruction by shepherds as stupid as themselves. I thought of my passion for universal justice, of my desire that all men should be free, leisured, educated, of my imaginations of a future earth peopled by human beings who should live according to reason. ... And this war, I thought. Was there the slightest prospect that any good would come of it? The war to end war! The argument was forcible enough this time; it was backed up with a kick in the breech, the most terrific kick ever administered. But would it convince humanity more effectively than any other argument had ever done?"

Then he thinks that, for all that, men are courageous, kind, patient and self-sacrificing and do not mean to be bad; on which the only comment he can make is, "Forgive them for they know not what they do." He thinks of the few who are intelligently aware, but decides that they are merely odd exceptions, irrelevant to the fundamental reality that this world in which we live is stupid. They are more lies, like the ideal of love, or his own quondam belief in justice. The whole episode, within the context of Chelifer's melancholy autobiography, is a vivid picture of the disillusion of the Twenties.

It is also a perfect example of what I have called Huxley's hypnosis. Ideas are inserted in our minds; we want eagerly to argue about them: to say, for instance, that Chelifer is an ass who thinks that reality gives the lie direct to imagination merely because his silly fantasy has given the lie direct to nature; or to point out that because a girl prefers to be the trollop that she is rather than the angel somebody chooses to think her is no reason for enlarging misanthropically on the world in general. That we may wish to argue so is a tribute to the author. We cannot, however, attribute total responsibility for Chelifer's ideas to Huxley, nor even go so far as to say that he has had no right to compose the sequence with feelings of compassion or pity for Chelifer. This is, in theory, Chelifer himself weeping over his own wounded heart. All we can legitimately say is that the author, aware of the foolishness of Chelifer, must before the novel ends deploy him in a fitting manner, give him the fate which, with his own life-view, he considers appropriate for such folly. Does he do so? As we have seen, Chelifer's fate is that he cannot escape from the votes of the masses as to the nature of reality, and that their view of life bores and disgusts him. "One has no right," he says, "to ignore what for every ninety-nine out of every hundred human beings is reality—even though it mayn't actually be the real thing." He even says: "If you

want to know what human life is you must be courageous and
live as the majority of human beings actually do live. It's
singularly revolting, I assure you." The only explicit comment
Huxley makes on this, through one of his (ambiguous) mouth-
pieces, is to suggest to us that Chelifer is an inverted senti-
mentalist; one, that is, who instead of seeing everything in a
rosy light gloats over horrors; but it may strike us as a more
adequate judgement on Chelifer that his folly leads him in
the end to the death of all pleasure, all joy in life. This *accedia*
is Huxley's usual punishment for his characters. From the
viewpoint of the Twenties it is the most cruel of all punishments.
They knew the misery of boredom all too well.

   Whose the fault? Their own? Or the "wearisome condition of
humanity"? Huxley, it seems to this reader, here plays the part
of jesting Pilate. Everything he has written in this period is, like
Mr Mercaptan's "Loves of the Pachyderms", "all very witty and
delicately savage", but as for general conclusions, one may seek
for them—indeed, as I have intimated, one is somehow led to
expect them—but after one has discovered that one is not going
to get them one ceases to ask for them any longer. And how
could they arise in any novel about a groping period by a man
who was evidently groping himself? *The Slough of Despond*:
wittily described in several volumes by One Who Knows.

   Too much has been left out for conclusions to arise: chiefly
such elementary matters as the knowledge of good and evil.
These characters are all in a strange dilemma: they have eaten
of the apple, but like those curious early Oriental Gnostics
known as the Naasseni who sang hymns of praise to the serpent
of transgression, the knowledge they have acquired has taught
them nothing either about good or about evil. They have
learned only about the results of certain kinds of behaviour
to which they give no moral names. And their ultimate reactions
are, as it happens, very like those of the Gnostics who wavered

between the hatred of matter and the embrace of matter according to their temperaments. Inevitably they have no philosophy, and any novel about them must be without any central figure to represent any satisfactory system of thought, or indeed any satisfactory system of behaviour. Being all rebels or martyrs–there is no hero–happiness can only come to them momentarily. As Mrs Quarles says to Marjorie Carling with characteristic Huxleyan wit: "Happiness is like coke–something you get as a by-product in the process of making something else."

As parables the novels are fair pictures of the Twenties; or, if one prefers, fair caricatures. I am not at all sure that one is entitled to ask if they áre fair pictures, or caricatures, of life in general, then or at any time, but if one does ask, then one must say that they certainly–one may be so downright–are not. They are too absolute. That characters cut to the bone to represent absolute positions lose the complexity of human nature one may not mind, since these are novels of ideas not of character; but it is fatal to the universal application of these parables that characters who lack the complexity of human nature must, perforce, also oversimplify the questions they are intended to project.

Why is it that we relished these novels when they first appeared more than we do today? (One does not speak of an uncritical relish at either time; one can be critical and enjoy all the more for that; but today the enjoyment is quite different in that it is now devoid of the quality of glee which distinguished it in those years.) I can here only give my own feelings: which seem, when I examine them, to close in on a point which I raised early on: Huxley's detachment. I find that I form reservations about it amounting to an uncomfortable fear that it inadequately conceals that form of self-pity precisely defined by the author when speaking of Chelifer's inverted sentimentality which makes him, in wishing that the world were other than it is, concentrate on its most unpleasant elements. This form of sentimentality might be described as the feelings of a man, part-aesthete, part-Puritan, looking into a distorting mirror of life with a groan and a grimace. And this excess of Augustinian sensibility induces further reservations with regard to Huxley's integrity at this period of his development. If a writer chooses to stand on his head nobody can object provided he does not pretend that he is not standing on his head. If Huxley is without ambiguity setting out solely to entertain us (using the word on the highest level) his pose, posture or approach is largely his own affair, though we will, as a matter of course, take note of these things if for no other reason than to decide how seriously he wishes to be taken. It may seem, however, that there is a certain amount of double-shuffle in these novels. The author is an entertainer, but he is also an intellectual in the dictionary's sense of "a member of a class or group professing, or supposed to possess, enlightened judgement and opinions with respect to public or political questions". That sentimental streak to which I refer has begun to vitiate for me Huxley's detachment, and so his integrity and, finally, his intelligence. These early novels, while they remain entertaining parables, now appear to have been based on a wholly personal view of life which I do not find sufficiently inclusive to call intelligent. The impression a re-reading of these novels gives one today is of an arid and desiccated waste, bordering at many points on jungles of odorous despair, always blessedly watered by a constant dew of bitter wit and otherwise illuminated not by intelligence but by brilliant intellectual pyrotechnics.

It is possible to perceive several other reasons why this should be the effect of the passage of time. Two seem to be more plausible than others. For one thing, these novels were topical novels in the sense in which Shaw's plays were often topical plays, and with changing conditions the ideas lose much of their

appeal. Nowadays Huxley is most topical when he is discussing
not contemporary society but the past and the future, and one
will agree that history and prophecy are realms in which the
imagination is least liable to be given the lie by reality. With
this goes the fact that the spirit of the Twenties, which produced
and once responded so gleefully to the novels, is gone or quite
altered. It was natural then to be sorry for oneself, to express
one's disgust with the wearisome condition of humanity either
by being puritanical or the reckless opposite, one's disbelief in
society by denying sin and misdoubting virtue, one's contempt
for traditional solutions by posing abstract questions to which
one knew there was no real answer, to take refuge from the
world in aestheticism, to show one's distrust of all large political
conclusions by finding the hero-type only in the lone wolf—
D. H. and T. E. Lawrence were the ideal hero-types of the
era—because honesty and idealism could have no validity except
for the individual or the very few. The uplifted right arms of
the three dictators put an end to all that. Today we huddle, and
listen uncomfortably to the not too hopeful prophets. But,
leaving the times out of it altogether, how could they be
hopeful? They never had been. Orwell, Koestler, Eliot,
Huxley. . . . One closes one's eyes at the thought that one of
these days Mr Graham Greene may decide to announce the
future of the race.

Waugh's detachment, while having its own shape of ambiguity, is much more genuine than Huxley's. He is detached
by hardness of mind, hardness of thought about people—not
about affairs, or ideas, for he is not in any sense an intellectual;
he is, or rather was in his great satirical period, a man of fashion
with Joyce's trick of suddenly leaving the company to take
satirical notes on his cuff in the wash-room. Where this
toughness springs from God (quite literally) alone knows:

it was one of those inexplicable natural gifts like genius or personality.

It must have helped that he early became a Roman Catholic. (Many critics who do not warm to the Catholic feeling in *Brideshead Revisited* seem to forget that Waugh had become converted to Catholicism in the year of the publication of his second novel.) For to be a Catholic in England is to be detached by many degrees from the main English tradition.

"The aesthetic appeal of the Church of England [Waugh himself X wrote] is unique and peculiar to these islands. . . . In England the . . . mediaeval cathedrals and churches, the rich ceremonies that surround the monarch, the historic titles of Canterbury and York, the social organization of the country parishes, the traditional culture of Oxford and Cambridge, the liturgy composed in the hey-day of English prose-style—all these are the property of the Church of England, while Catholics meet in modern buildings, often of deplorable design, and are usually served by simple Irish missionaries."

Does one imagine a note of nostalgia, which would imply attachment-detachment, and promise sympathy and under-standing? I cannot help recalling Newman after his conversion saying sadly to a fellow-convert that his new friends had never known the world in which he, in memory, still lived.

Then there is the class-difference. A critic once described him as a snob and he replied: "I think perhaps he is right in calling me a snob; that is to say, I am happiest in the company of the European upper classes." Happy, but possibly also all the more objective about them by not having been born into them. His grandfather was a country doctor from Somerset; his father, after Sherborne and New College, became a reader to Kegan Paul, later chairman of Chapman and Hall, a prolific editor of the English classics. It is, in the good French sense, a bourgeois background. When Evelyn Waugh passed through

Lancing and Hertford College he moved into a wider world, a step which it is not so easy to take in France as in England; unless one can equate the Jockey Club with St James's and Buck's–Waugh's clubs–as open doors to the life of "the European upper classes"?

And there was his formative period, with its critical attitude to life in general and English life in particular. Had he been born fifteen years earlier or later he might have been led to join the Labour Party. (It may not sound likely; but one remembers that Wellington, Balliol and the Foreign Office could lead so sceptical a mind as the Hon. Harold Nicolson's that way.) The kind of party that attracted Waugh's contemporaries led him to *Vile Bodies*.

"Masked parties. Savage parties. Victorian parties, Greek parties, Wild West parties, Russian parties, Circus parties, parties where one had to dress as somebody else, almost naked parties in Saint John's Wood, parties in flats and studios and houses and ships and hotels and night clubs, in windmills and swimming-baths, tea parties at school where one ate muffins and meringues and tinned-crab, parties at Oxford where one drank brown sherry and smoked Turkish cigarettes, dull dances in London and comic dances in Scotland and disgusting dances in Paris–all that succession and repetition of massed humanity. ... Those vile bodies. ..."

Even this brief run, culminating in the title of the novel, so characteristic of Waugh's style in its eclectic adjective, proposes a very different kind of mind to Huxley's, for though it inveighs it does it with gusto, and one reads it not in admiring glee at the destruction wrought but with an amusement unalloyed by contempt for its victims. The adjective alone might put us at our ease, like a reliable name on an aircraft; we feel we are taking off with a good company in good company. *Vile* has no sour connotations. It is not depressing, it is not moral, it is young and lively and it is also old and reputable, a blend of

Shakespeare and slang; it suggests a sort of hopeless, good-humoured scorn of fate, chance or folly like a man who has gone for a long tramp in vile weather with a leaking mackintosh, and will describe his misfortunes afterwards with a blend of resignation and derision which does not exclude the suggestion that he enjoyed the adventure he reviles. Attachment-detachment again?

The effect of this genuine but ambiguous detachment of Waugh's is that the laughter his first six novels evoke is our happy tribute to the delicate balance he strikes between his detachment from his characters which allows him to satirise them and his affection for them which allows him to pity them. Surely we all remember *Vile Bodies* as much for its compassion as its bite? Recall, for example, how generously he handles those two vile bodies Adam and Nina. They are a foolish young couple and he does not spare them the exposure of their folly, but he never suggests that they are wicked, and he does not moralise over them. They did anticipate their wedding-night, but they loved one another truly; and as if to alleviate their unorthodox behaviour Waugh so arranges things that Adam intended to anticipate lawful wedlock only by one night, and that Nina yielded to him only because she was so touched by his silly dance of joy over the cheque he had extracted from her dotty father that she could not bear to point out to him that her papa had signed it with the name Charlie Chaplin. He grants them virtues, however foolishly applied, as when he allows them to visit the sick–Miss Runcible–though so boisterously that their kindness helps to polish her off. He does not spare them their choice of friends. Peter Pastmaster drinks like a fish and sleeps with negresses; Lady Metroland is a high-class procuress; Miles Malpractice is a homosexual; Mrs Panrast is a Lesbian. But these are minor characters in the romance of Adam and Nina, and no society has ever been free of such aberrants. He makes Adam try to earn a living on which to marry Nina, though because he is an incompetent young fool he must be dogged by bad luck and always look like a silly young mug. Adam is entirely faithful to Nina and when he marries her we are to presume that they live happily ever after. Indeed, the unique thing about *Vile Bodies* is that this satire by an undeceived contemporary has achieved so much benevolence without an iota of sentimentality.

But, then, Waugh is sometimes charged with unnecessary cruelty towards his characters? Mr Donat O'Donnell, for example, writes in his interesting study of a group of Catholic novelists, *Maria Cross*:

"Mr Waugh is a great explorer of human disadvantages, and his unscrupulous adolescent cruelty in this is the common quality of his two most obvious characteristics: his humour and his snobbery. Two of his comic novels, *Black Mischief* and *Scoop*, are largely based on a sly appeal to the white man's sense of racial superiority; much of the best fun in *Decline and Fall* comes from the exploitation of Captain Grimes who, although he claimed to be a public school man, was not really a gentleman and did not often have a bath; in *Put Out More Flags* the purest comedy lies in the lurid descriptions of the appearance and behaviour of three proletarian children."

One must agree that Waugh does, frequently, indulge in pointless cruelty, and that when he does so it is a mistake and a blemish. In *Black Mischief* Mr Youkoumian treats his wife with such persistent and callous brutality that instead of laughing at her misfortunes we protest at them. But this is not usual with Waugh, and I think Mr O'Donnell has here missed two points, one essential to an understanding of Waugh; and I can only hope that it may make him feel a little uncomfortable to recall that G. K. Chesterton, who thought that the disasters piled on the innocent head of the hero of *Decline and Fall* were merely "distressing", would be entirely on his side.

First: while it is true that the misfortunes of Mrs Youkoumian are not funny, one must understand the analeptic mechanism of the sort of laughter they can produce. Some years ago a multiple murderer named John Christie was arrested, tried and hanged in London. He had enticed women into his flat, in the sort of quarter which would have been suitable for a Graham Greene or a Simenon crime story. He had strangled the women and stacked them up in a cupboard like coats on coat-hangers, one in front of the other. Others he had buried. I have heard this case discussed not only by intellectuals but by ordinary, good-living, decent Irish people with peals of laughter. In Dublin he was commonly referred to as Corpus Christie. Before that a man named Haigh had melted down several women in barrels of acid so that nothing was left in the bottom of the barrels but their false teeth. It was the only way by which one victim was identified. In the effort to escape the gallows Haigh not only pretended lunacy but declared that he drank his own urine. This also I have heard discussed with the utmost gaiety. Surely this sort of laughter is like a man who has drunk poison tickling his throat with a feather to make himself vomit the evil thing. Waugh is not, I feel, in his scenes of apparently gratuitous cruelty laughing at humanity, or laughing with humanity. His laughter is a horrible cathartic laughter. He invents a scape-goat who suffers the cruelty of life for us. We identify ourselves with the sufferer. We laugh it off. This does not make it funny. It does make it bearable. We have considered, faced-up to cruelty and borne it by proxy in some form, to some degree.

But Waugh's cruelty is more often a deliberate and well-pointed and wholly admirable part of his technique, and if it is double-edged it is for sound reasons. This is where Mr O'Donnell has not only missed a point but completely failed to understand what Waugh is generally driving at in his satires. True, the loathsome Mr Basil Seal does make money during the war by

packing dirty and destructive refugees into the gracious,
well-loved, much tended country homes of his neighbours,
later withdrawing them for handsome bribes. But what is
Waugh's purpose in this? Basil Seal is a type consistently
despised by the Twenties; a man without an iota of the admirable Epicurean private virtues they admired, and he is therefore
clearly presented as a crook. On the other hand, the soft-headed,
soft-boiled mugs whom he defrauded and tormented were
largely the people who, by their soft-headed goodness, had
brought all the trouble on the world in 1914; just as in the post-
war decade they would be going around, still mugs, still soft-
headed, asking people to sign peace pledges; just as later, in the
Thirties these same people would be reading Auden, and
Isherwood, and Spender, and Koestler and all the Pylon boys
who were the intellectual vanguard of the Socialist revolution
which would go far to wipe out the bourgeoisie completely–and
would have done so if there were not in even the softest-headed
British bourgeois some tough residue of the strain of Hampden
and of Pym that not even the half-baked Liberalism of the
nineteenth century and the inhuman humanism of the first
decades of the twentieth could wholly destroy. Waugh could
not possibly have been on the side of these deluded souls, even
against Seal. He regarded them much as a sergeant-major might
regard a thoroughly hopeless set of raw recruits; and he let
them "have it".

Besides, the Basil Seals of the world had at least three virtues
in the eyes of the Twenties: he was clever; and amusing–
"amusing" is still a popular word among English intellectuals,
applicable to anything from Byzantine Art to Boston Baked
Beans–and he was not contributing to the complacency of the
stupid good. He was therefore a useful Attila, a Scourge of God
to lash the stupid good and carry off his wickedness in scornful
laughter. It is almost always so in Waugh's novels. His

hard-bitten scoundrels surpass his heroes and heroines : Basil Seal, Margot Beste-Chetwynde who becomes Lady Metroland, Captain Grimes, Solomon Philbrick. Virtuous innocence is his laughing-stock, personified by any of Seal's pathetic victims, or Paul Pennyfeather, or Adam Symes, or old Prendergast, or Cedric Lyne, or Tony Last whose only fault was that he was a dull husband who did not know the ropes, and lived in an innocent (but to Waugh dangerous) dream of Gothic Worlds with dappled unicorns on the lawn, and childish toys senti-mentally preserved in the bedroom cupboard—just the sort of fellow who would become a hero in a silly war like that just finished in 1918.

It is interesting to compare him in this with Marcel Aymé. One knows from *Le Confort Intellectuel* where Aymé's sympathies lie, but from his novels, if one did not know that whom the Lord loves he punishes, one might be puzzled to decide where his loyalties lie. They lie, one then sees, with the backbone of French life as Aymé sees things, the bourgeois tradition, once solidly dependable, now become fuddled, corrupt, frightened, vain, and making an arrant fool of itself in its pursuit of all sorts of wrong ideas. This is why he lacerates the bourgeois family in *Travelingue*; their foolish, foppish gabble about the latest films, the nit-wit daughters' disreputable guests, the father toiling, the mother squandering. It adds up to a moralist's picture with the same sort of effect as Waugh's savagery in sending the proletariat children of the London slums down into the half-timbered, lawn-shaven, brass-gleaming homes of the bewildered, well-meaning, fat-headed bourgeoisie of England. In *Le Chemin des Ecoliers*, likewise, Aymé piles misfortune on the heads of Michaud and Lolivier, good, honest, simple men, but so unwise, so sentimental, so unshrewd. (The novel is a revealing commentary on our notion of the agate-headed, tough-minded, calculating, vulpine French business-man.)

Sentimentality is also the crime of Archambaud and Leopold in *Uranus*; they pay dearly for it, while the village boys literally get away with murder. But for the Fifties as for the Twenties the first commandment is: Thou shalt not be soft-headed or soft-hearted, because that way lies evil and death. Aymé, like Waugh, seems to be saying, challengingly: Be clever, sweet child, and let who will be good. Basil Seal's refugee children, then, in *Put Out More Flags*, are not funny, nor intended to be funny, but the triumph of wickedness (Basil Seal's) over virtue is first-class satire. These hideous children are evil's knout.

Both in Aymé and in Waugh the mask of virtue is ripped away, and other masks. "Thus he would watch in the asparagus season a dribble of melted butter on a woman's chin, marring her beauty and making her look ridiculous, while she would still talk and smile and turn her head, not knowing how she appeared to him." "Her make-up was haphazard and garish, rather like a later Utrillo." Somebody else's war-paint is "sploshy, like a John portrait". But it is an impartial process. Even Saint Helena is made tolerable only by being presented as a Miserere Mei in her youth and a bit of a fool in her old age. We remember her reply to the Holy Father when she told him that she was going off to find the True Cross. "You will tell me, will you not," he says with the gentlest irony, "if you are successful?" She cries, "I'll tell the world!" One notes, however, that there is no venom in the unmasking, no bitter hate. One of Waugh's pet aversions is the higher intellectual. He does not rend the creature; he is content to describe his miserable surroundings, his dreary flat, his bath-water oozing sadly from that Edwardian collection of verdigris-green viscera called the hot-water geyser which at best gives a niggardly trickle of warm water and at worst explodes in clouds of poisonous vapour. He permits himself only one brief and impartial comment: "But apparatus of this nature is the hallmark of the higher intellectual the world over." He pulls the legs of Catholics when Ambrose Silk, disguised as an Irish priest, is fleeing to Ireland. "Have you a breviary?" his friend asks, examining the disguise for verisimilitude in details. Ambrose says he has not. His friend says, "Oh, well, then, be reading a racing paper!" But the really important unmasking is that of the life of the young people of his decade whom he presents not so much with paternal bitterness as with brotherly exasperation, always assuaged—or so one may feel—by his honest memory of how much he enjoyed their company while the going was good. For all through his work the sub-audible implications suggest certain foiled desires, certain ideals, a certain norm which, he feels, their lives denied, so that one gradually begins to see that his way of presenting them involves what music-hall comedians call the Double Take. We laugh, and then the rubber-band slaps back in our faces and we realise that the laugh is on us. While he is making us laugh over the follies of these young people, even inducing in us some sympathy with their rebellion against their elders, their general disillusion, their dissatisfaction with what Miss Elizabeth Bowen has called the "edited" life of conventional society, we begin to realise that Waugh is also revealing that he is disillusioned over their disillusionment and rebelling against their revolt. He is seeing through them just as clearly as he insists on seeing through a garish make-up. He sees that their revolt is negative, their lives are prodigal, they are just as incapable of any clear concept of a desirable image or way of life as their fathers against whom they are in revolt. That scene in which Miss Runcible dies while all her gay friends sit around her bed cracking jokes, exchanging gossip and drinking champagne, unaware that she is sinking into oblivion, could be taken as a symbol of Waugh's basically moral criticism of the Twenties, whose kiss is death.

It is not that there is anything much that is positively wrong

about them; it is that their lives are fatally negative. As we
watch them we may feel side-by-side with Hemingway in
The Sun Also Rises which comments in the same spirit on the
American expatriates in Paris and Spain between 1918 and the
Depression. These amusing, often delightful young people of
Waugh's satires were not without their own earnestness, their
own longings, their own idealism, but, to borrow from Camus's
L'Homme Revolté, they can only gyrate in the realm of rebellion,
incoherently, emotionally, without ever advancing into the
realm of those ideas which belong to creative revolt. So they
waste life, managing it so loosely. Their damnation is a depriva-
tion, an absence, a vacuity, like Marlowe's hell. In those wild
days and nights of the Twenties it must have sometimes occurred
to Waugh as it did to Lawrence that they were all "done for",
that at any moment the clock would strike and the chorus come
in chanting to the jazz-drums of falling bombs and clattering
ack-ack,

> *Cut is the branch that might have grown full straight*
> *And burned is Apollo's laurel bough.*

In his early and, I think, best books Waugh said none of
this–he was much too finely equilibrated a humorist to utter
explicit statements, and so long as he could imply his norm he
apparently felt no urge to project a positive hero to represent it.
This reticence delighted his generation and continues to delight
us, as it will probably delight every generation to come. It is
the mark of the moral satirist who, like all universal moralists,
has detached himself from the accidentals of life by withdrawing
to the remote ground of principles so general that–as I have
suggested by the comparison with the novels of Marcel Aymé–
they could be equally acceptable to people of another nation,
and of another time.

This admirable detachment disappeared with the publication

of *Brideshead Revisited* in which Mr Waugh changed ground.
Ceasing to be a moral satirist he became a writer of romances.
We, his devoted readers, had to make, and were not always
able to make, a rapid adjustment of our expectations, and, if
we were his critics, were called on to apply totally different
standards. At this distance it is easier to do both things; to
recognise that this is not (to understate) another funny book,
that it is solemn and serious, romantic and nostalgic, exclusive
and personal, and, far from being general in its application,
relies to a most disturbing degree on its appeal to our interest
through accidental and irrelevant detail. It is this last point
which strikes one the most forcibly; as may be seen at once if
we retell the story without the accidentals.

One Charles Ryder meets a young man named Flyte, and
through him his family. The father and mother have separated.
They had both been religious-minded people, the mother being
specially pious, but the father abandoned his religion when he
left his wife to live with his mistress. The mother dies midway
through the book. There are four children. Young Flyte and his
sister Julia have reacted from their mother; his brother and his
sister remain close to her. Flyte becomes a dipsomaniac, driven
to drink, one might say, by the insistent morality of his mother.
Julia marries a thrusting Canadian, outside the church of her
origin, has an affair with somebody unnamed, falls in love with
Ryder and proceeds to divorce her Canadian husband. When
the father ultimately returns home to die, Julia is so affected by
seeing him, at the point of his final coma, bless himself that she
refuses to marry Ryder, breaks off the proposed marriage, and,
we are to understand, returns to the religion of her parents.
Ryder, an agnostic, is impressed and begins to take an interest
in religion. When the war breaks out the old home is taken over
by the military. A rather conventional romance.

Such a summary, like all summaries, cannot, of course, even

remotely suggest the manner in which Waugh has treated his
story, or the sort of life he has infused into these bare bones:
it does help to define a subject which a dozen writers might
treat in a dozen different ways. But Waugh has written his story
in a mood of such nostalgic heart-ache for old things passing or
passed away, in a style so tender and fondling, given his chief
characters such picturesque backgrounds and so much inherited
wealth and traditional grace that one could not quarrel, even
while one winced, with Miss Rose Macaulay's choice of the
word "lushness" to describe the general effect of surfeit. It
would be unjust not to say that he also showed that he possessed
hitherto unexpected technical resources for the handling of
extended scenes and complex moods: to give only one instance,
the swift sketching-in of Ryder's relationship with his wife,
and the unstated but clearly felt suggestion of his own state of
mind at the beginning of Book Two is a masterly development
of the old quickie technique of disconnected snapshots. Indeed
the chief development in this novel is from disjunction to
smoothness—perhaps too much smoothness. Yet, technique
apart, how much of his treatment of the essential subject
amounts to unessential trappings! It is quite irrelevant, to give
a dozen examples, that young Flyte is Lord Sebastian Flyte; that
he is a lovely, epicene young man of the Nineties with engagingly
eccentric ways, such as his devotion to his teddy-bear Aloysius;
that he and Ryder meet amid the golden glories of Oxford; that
his father is a marquis, his home a beautiful country house, and
that he lives now with an Italian mistress in a Venetian palace;
that Julia is Lady Julia, or that she marries a man who becomes a
Cabinet Minister; that her love affair with Ryder begins aboard
a liner, First Class, during a storm, in the environment of roses,
masseuse-oil and champagne; that Lord Sebastian becomes a
dipsomaniac not among the pubs of Camden Town but in the
low dives of Fez. All this is romantic embroidery; a harmless

pleasure for the reader, just as it is a pleasure to listen to well-bred people talking in a well-dressed play about something else besides the mist that does be on the bog, or fish-and-chips or Rearmament, moral or otherwise. But when we have passed through these accidentals to what seems at first sight to be the core of the novel, its insistently pervasive Catholicism, it is with a shock of dismay that we gradually realise that this is the most irrelevant accidental of all. In fact, if I may be permitted to give my own personal reaction to the novel as a professing Catholic (adding in all humility that there may be something wrong with my idea of Catholicism), I fail to see why the book could not have been equally well written–admittedly with a very different setting–by a fervent Congregationalist. Had, for instance, the author of *Mark Rutherford's Autobiography* written *Brideshead Revisited* as *Tanner's Lane Revisited* we might not only have been just as impressed, but perhaps more deeply impressed had he done with it what he did with the *Autobiography*, that is, turned the accidental or immediate subject of his inherited faith into the universal theme of any man's struggles and tensions with any religious dogma whatsoever. This seems to be the essential question. Does Waugh universalise his theme, or does he move within an enclosed and exclusive circle of very limited appeal?

What is his theme? If it is that there is no happiness on earth without God no member of any theistic religion would deny it. If it is that God lures us back to him by ways obscure and strange a Mohammedan would not deny it. If it is the "twitch on the thread" which can pull men back from the ends of the earth, from the deepest jungles of indifference and vice to the ways of virtue, the validity of the observation is almost devastatingly universal. It applies to so many pulls, such as patriotism and love. It may, for all one knows, work powerfully with the Salvation Army. Any novel dealing with any of these

themes, and they all occur in *Brideshead Revisited*, must, if it
proposes to show how they operate inside one particular religion,
throw a piercing light on the specific quality, power and appeal
of that religion, or show them operating in such a way as to
impress equally an atheist, an agnostic or a member of any
Church in the world. Otherwise, obviously, its appeal is not
universal. My feeling is that Waugh has not fully succeeded in
doing either of these things, and for the reason I have stated – that
he has abandoned his detachment, to which I would here add
that he has abandoned it through an excess of loyalty.

For the first, would, say, a Mohammedan reading the novel
understand the power and the appeal of Catholicism? He
would certainly have to acknowledge its power, since it is so
clearly stated – which is not the same thing as to understand it.
Its emotional appeal he could not possibly understand. Even I,
who happen to be a Catholic, fail to see the appeal of any such
religion as is here depicted, if for no other reason than that it
has brought the minimum of happiness to the maximum number
of people; and I do not speak of happiness in a worldly sense.
Nor can it be argued that the lives of the Marquis, Lord Sebastian
or Lady Julia show that if Catholics are unhappy it is only
because they do not practise their religion. The mother is a
devout Catholic: she appears throughout as a most melancholy
woman who is hated by her husband and who has driven her
son to drink. Her elder son, Brideshead, also a devout Catholic,
is as sombre a figure as one would willingly take a day's march
to avoid. To Cordelia, the younger daughter, religion is indeed a
tower of strength and consolation and our Mohammedan reader
must feel that a faith so powerful to console and bestow inner
joy is something to envy. But the most contented person of all
is Cara, the mistress of the Marquis, who has learned in the
light-hearted Italian way to wear her religion easily and rely
on the infinite goodness of God. If Mr Waugh were writing

propaganda for the Catholic Church she is the woman most
likely of all to convert our heathen friend. (Why does everybody
who writes about religion concentrate on being miserable
about it?)

The theme, as we have seen, is universally valid; the treatment
is not. In effect it is reduced from godliness to obedience.
Consider the turning-point in the whole story, which is centrally
the story of Charles Ryder and Julia Flyte. It occurs when
Brideshead is telling Ryder and his sister of his intention to
marry a Catholic widow; referring to his sister's marriage,
outside the church, to the divorced Canadian Rex Mottram,
he says roughly that his future wife would not possibly live
in the same house as Julia: "It is a matter of indifference whether
you choose to live in sin with Rex or Charles or both–I have
always avoided inquiry into the details of your *ménage*–but
in no case would Beryl consent to be your guest." The result
of this bombshell is a harrowing emotional outbreak from
Julia in a long speech delivered to Ryder, alone, on the subject
of her sin:

"All in one word, too, one little, flat, deadly word that covers a
lifetime.

"'Living in sin'; not just doing wrong, as I did when I went to
America; doing wrong, knowing it is wrong, stopping doing it,
forgetting. That's not what they mean. That's not Bridey's penny-
worth. He means just what it says in black and white.

"*Living in sin*, with sin, by sin, for sin, every hour, every day,
year in and year out. Waking up with sin in the morning, slipping
diamonds to it, feeding it, showing it round, giving it a good time,
putting it to sleep at night with a tablet of Dial if its fretful.

"Always the same, like an idiot child carefully nursed, guarded
from the world. 'Poor Julia,' they say, 'she can't go out. She's got
to take care of her little sin. A pity it ever lived,' they say, 'but it's so
strong. Children like that always are. Julia's so good to her little,
mad sin.'"

Then her speech rises to a wild threnody for Christ dying with
her sin, over the bed in the night-nursery, in the dark little
study at Farm Street with the shining oil-cloth, in dark churches
where the charwoman's brush is raising dust and one candle
burns; and so on to the thought of a never-to-be-comforted
Christ, a Christ never given shelter, always hanging there,
outcast, a Citizen of the bare stone and the dust and the smoulder-
ing dumps, thrown away there, poked at after nightfall by an
old man with lupus carrying a forked stick, "nameless and dead,
like the baby they wrapped up and carried away before I had
seen her". The scene ends with her lashing her agnostic lover
across the face with a switch because he has said something that
she thinks stupid and lacking in sympathy and understanding.
It is a painful and impressive scene. Yet, what was this frightful
sin? To everybody except to Roman Catholics or High
Anglicans divorce is specifically a Roman Catholic sin; a sin
of disobedience; a theological sin; a sin against the Council
of Trent; a sin argued about over many centuries; an institutional
sin; a club sin. They will feel deeply for Julia, but they will
also feel like outsiders looking in. They must feel this even
more during those long, professional arguments, at the end,
when Marchmain is dying, about the efficacy of Extreme
Unction for a semi-conscious, if not virtually unconscious,
man.

A religious theme given institutional treatment is always liable
to get lost in the embroidered folds of ecclesiasticism; and so is
the author. The old detachment is sold to loyalty, and while
one admires loyalty there is no place for it in art, just as there
is no place for it in philosophy—or for that matter in mathe-
matics. The team-spirit breeds loyalty, but artists and philo-
sophers (and mathematicians) do not work in teams. In reading
Brideshead one wrings one's hands when Waugh's loyalty to the
aristocratic spirit makes him say of the family history given to

Ryder by Lady Marchmain–a "family history typical of the Catholic squires of England": "These men must die to make a world for Hooper; they were the aborigines, vermin by right of law, to be shot off at leisure so that things might be safe for the travelling salesman, with his polygonal pince-nez, his fat wet hand-shake, his grinning dentures"–Hooper being the harmless representative in this novel of the cruder post-war world nowadays satirised by writers like Mr John Wain and Mr Kingsley Amis. The point is not that one disagrees or agrees with Waugh about the superiority of the Catholic squires of England to the non-Catholic salesmen of England; the point is that this is not the snarling way for any man of letters, least of all for so gifted a satirist, to make any point whatever. One must only feel that in *Brideshead*, whether dealing with Church or class, Waugh has allowed himself to be drawn into the whirlpool of his subject. He became his own Undine, killing with a kiss. The moralist, losing his detached standpoint, died, and so did his satire. Where the changeling Waugh went to nobody knows, but he cannot really be far away: he has returned with *The Loved One* and some splendid sequences in his last two novels.

Yet, here again loyalties dominate, and he is again arguing against himself. His natural, instinctive, inherited position was that those same times which destroyed the traditional nobility eliminated the traditional hero. Hungry for both, he has concentrated in *Men at Arms* and *Officers and Gentlemen* on the professional hero (as in *Brideshead* on the professional Catholic) who is, it is quite true, a well-known and highly-valued type in the British Army: the well-bred, utterly loyal, utterly fearless Catholic public-schoolman. Apart from the fact that the area is once again as enclosed and circumscribed as a Henty novel, Waugh's loyalty in response to loyalty is seen to be patiently excessive and destructive of detachment by the fact that all his

wealth of satire is reserved for commoners and there is not a
glimmer of humour in his picture of Guy Crouchback, who,
by a shift of angle, such as Stendhal commanded, must appear
as a character with endless comic possibilities. It does not even
seem to occur to him that from the point of view, and in the
language of Crouchback's fellow-officers and superiors, he must
have often appeared as a pain-in-the-neck. It must be that
although there is room and room enough for humour on the
subject of loyalty, humour is another one of those pursuits in
which there is no room for loyalty. But few humorists have a
sense of humour about everything. Most have no sense of
humour about themselves.

Waugh is a writer of a purely brainless genius, which he has
amplified by the possession or development of enormous
technical skill. He was born with the natural gift for satire.
His satires will probably live as long as literature lasts. And he
has written seven of them! What an achievement that is one
may realise by trying to think offhand of seven other comic
novels by seven other individual English writers. Being a man
of genius he should never, under any circumstances, have
opinions, for whenever he has written out of his opinions it
becomes all too plain all over again that imagination is a
soaring gull and opinions no more than a gaggle of ungainly
starlings, chattering angrily on a cornfield. Opinions breed
anger, nourish hate, ossify the heart, narrow the mind.

> *An intellectual hatred is the worst,*
> *So let her think opinions are accursed.*
> *Have I not seen the loveliest woman born*
> *Out of the mouth of Plenty's horn,*
> *Because of her opinionated mind*
> *Barter that horn and every good*
> *By quiet natures understood*
> *For an old bellows full of angry wind?*

He has what Yeats wished for his daughter, a "radical innocence . . . self-delighting, self-appeasing, self-affrighting". He
did not receive it from ancestry, or from this class or that, from
church or university; he did not build it out of ideas, or theories.
It is one of Nature's primal gifts. But it can be lost, and it can
commit suicide. It can poison itself. Thinking is pure poison
to innocence. Huxley who never knew innocence thrives on
thought. Waugh? One recalls what Cocteau said of Mistin-
guette, that she magnificently reversed Descartes's *Cogito, ergo
sum* into *Mais je ne pense jamais! Donc je suis!*

GRAHAM GREENE

or

I suffer, therefore I am

The two most striking things about the novels of Graham Greene are their preoccupation with evil and their intellectual *jusqu' au-boutisme*. As for the latter one is reminded of Camus's declaration that it is not sufficient to live, we must have and perceive a destiny that does not wait on death: man, that is, wants to anticipate his own destiny, and every writer wants to express in terms of this world the mortal destiny of man. It is a modern attitude among novelists. They were formerly satisfied to bring their novels to an intermediate destination rather than to expound an ultimate destiny. Marriage, love, domestic happiness, self-completion, self-fulfilment, self-perfection are in one way or another the themes of Balzac, Scott, Dickens, Stendhal and Tolstoy; whereas it has been well said that Greene, Mauriac and Bernanos return us to the medieval world, as if the great humanist tradition had never happened. Where Dante saw the totality of human destiny as a vision outside the flaming ramparts of the world, men like Greene bring the other world into this present life. If this has, as I intend to suggest, the effect of disintegrating his characters, of liquefying them, possibly of dehumanising them, it also has the fine effect of enlarging the imaginative and visionary content of his work. It explains, at any rate, his extremism, his reckless courage in taking an idea to the limits of its implications. (He does this nowhere more fully than in *The Heart of the Matter*.) It is something which fills the sensitive reader with apprehension. "Whither next?" one asks, and wonders when he will come up against a stone wall, or a chasm.

His obsession with the ugly and evil side of life is equally troubling. More than occasionally one feels that he is not merely outraging nature but that he is taking a perverse pleasure in rubbing its face in its own ordure. One feels that in concentrating on a restricted set of themes he has implied that no matter what subject he may choose to paint–childhood innocence, mother-love, a first kiss–he could make it look just as grim. Not, of course, that anybody has the least right to object to grimness, and every writer is entitled to wear whatever spectacles he pleases. But one may, indeed must if necessary, draw attention to the limitations of an artist's palette, or of his human sympathy, or of his intellectual interests. One may, if necessary, draw a distinction between an intellectual approach and a pathological obsession. I feel that more than a few of Greene's books justify our apprehension on all these counts; that his attitude to life exists, like the mental world of Pascal, so close to the border-line of the morbid and corrupt as to be saved from both only by the utmost delicacy and restraint; and much of Greene's work, to my mind, shows small signs that he is sufficiently aware of the importance of these sanitary precautions.

It must be clear to us all by now–he has made it clear–that his attraction to evil and ugliness was originally instinctive or emotional, and that he has gradually built about it an intellectual scaffolding. It is the natural way of the artist: first feeling, then perception. Evil and ugliness inspire him. They are the compost of his flower-garden. Faith, for him, is not a gift, it is won from Despair. Love relies on the validity of Hate. His hope of heaven

depends on the reality of hell. He believes in God because he
believes in Satan. That it is an uncomfortable and not very
attractive approach does not invalidate it; and it is not entirely
alien to the English tradition–one thinks at once of Bunyan.
Indeed there is nothing absolutely startling or new about it. Man
has always cried to the Lord *de profundis*, and moralists have
frequently observed that the most direct road to godliness may
be the road that seems to lead the other way. Pierre Emmanuel
said it simply in his *Autobiography* when he declared that it is
not morality but immorality (ugliness and evil) that brings us
to God–the nauseating experience of finding ourselves face
to face with our own naked shame and stale self-disgust. Yet
few writers have found so much positive satisfaction, even
comfort, in the sight of evil as Greene has. Joyfully he reverses
Browning. God's in his heaven, all's wrong with the world.
He *has* to be in his heaven. Conversely, whenever Greene sees
people happy in their vulgar, cheery, beery way he is filled with
gloom. No good, he seems to say, can possibly come of
happiness.

He has been explicit about this in the opening pages of *The
Lawless Roads*, that entirely dreary book about Mexico which,
in passing, is as good an illustration as any of his less successful
books of the danger of sticking too rigidly to a narrow point
of view. The first two pages of the book will suffice:

"I was, I suppose, thirteen years old. Otherwise why should I have
been there–in secret–on the dark croquet lawn? I could hear the
rabbit moving behind me, munching the grass in his hutch; an
immense building with small windows, rather like Keble College,
bounded the lawn. It was the school; from somewhere behind it,
from across the quad, came a faint sound of music: Saturday night,
the school orchestra was playing Mendelssohn. I was alone in mourn-
ful happiness in the dark. Two countries just here lay side by side.
From the croquet lawn, from the raspberry canes, from the green-
house and the tennis lawn you could always see–dominatingly–the

great square Victorian buildings of garish brick: they looked down like skyscrapers on a small green countryside where the fruit trees grew and the rabbits munched. You had to step carefully: the border was close beside your gravel path. From my mother's bedroom window–where she had borne the youngest of us to the sound of school-chatter and the disciplinary bell–you looked straight down into the quad, where the hall and the chapel and the classrooms stood. If you pushed open a green baize door in a passage by my father's study, you entered another passage deceptively similar, but none the less you were on alien ground. There would be a slight smell of iodine from the matron's room, of damp towels from the changing rooms, of ink everywhere. Shut the door behind you again, and the world smelt differently: books and fruit and eau-de-Cologne.

One was an inhabitant of both countries: on Saturday and Sunday afternoons on one side of the baize door, the rest of the week on the other. How can life on a border be other than restless? You are pulled by different ties, of hate and love. For hate is quite as powerful a tie: it demands allegiance. In the land of the skyscrapers, of stone stairs and cracked bells ringing early, one was aware of fear and hate, a kind of lawlessness–appalling cruelties could be practised without a second thought; one met for the first time characters, adult and adolescent, who bore about them the genuine quality of evil. There was Collifax who practised torments with dividers; Mr Cranden with three grim chins, a dusty gown, a kind of demoniac sensuality; from these heights evil declined towards Parlow, whose desk was filled with minute photographs–advertisements of art photos. Hell lay about them in their infancy."

One pauses at this parody of Wordsworth. Does "hate" demand "allegiance"? Surely there is a confusion of mind here. The *person or thing* one loves or hates may demand allegiance: school, drink, the object for which one longs or lusts. When a man says he must have love he means either that he must have somebody to love truly, or somebody with whom to fornicate; and to the one he must give "allegiance", but must he to the other? It is a curious, and I think revealingly obsessional, choice of word. The memory proceeds:

"There lay the horror and the fascination. One escaped surreptitiously for an hour at a time: unknown to frontier guards, one stood on the wrong side of the border looking back—one should have been listening to Mendelssohn, but instead one heard the rabbit restlessly cropping near the croquet hoops. It was an hour of release—and also an hour of prayer. One became aware of God with an intensity—time hung suspended—music lay on the air; anything might happen before it became necessary to join the crowd across the border. There was no inevitability anywhere . . . faith was almost great enough to move mountains . . . the great buildings rocked in the darkness.

"And so faith came to one—shapelessly, without dogma, a presence above a croquet lawn, something associated with violence, cruelty, evil across the way. One began to believe in heaven because one believed in hell. . . ."

It is fascinating, and it is frightening. Thereafter will the boy ever be able to do without "hell"? Will it become: "One believes in heaven *only* because one believes in hell?" Will everything that is not heaven have to become hell? It begins to seem so. For from there the memory goes on to give us a strange picture of a little country town in Hertfordshire set in pastoral country within a crescent of the Chiltern hills. I must have passed through, or paused at this rather pleasant-looking town a dozen times before, one afternoon, halting at one of the pubs for a drink, and observing a couple of men who were obviously schoolmasters chatting amiably over a beer, I realised that this was the hideous town anathematised in the opening pages of *The Lawless Roads*. Everything in Greene's description of it is in the manner of Joyce's impressions of a Dublin slum. Our attention is directed to a shabby shop selling *London Life*, with the usual "articles about high heels, corsets and long hair" (for men, one presumes); to the fake Tudor Café where four one-armed men dine together, "arranging their seats so that their arms shouldn't clash"—which, one may observe, most two-armed people also do; we are told about "Irish servant girls making assignations for a ditch"—and one wonders how could Greene know. The most seemingly innocent things are made to seem cheap or sinister. When a girl is observed cutting some branches off a tree she does so "with an expression abased and secretive". The saw "wails" through the wood. The photographs in a shop window become "yellowing faces", and they "peer out" at passers-by. When somebody pushes in the door of the Plough Inn it chimes; "... ivory balls clicked, and a bystander said, 'They do this at the Crown, Margate'—England's heart beating out in bagatelle to her eastern extremity". He quotes newspaper reports about a murder; about the suicide of a girl of fifteen, pregnant with a second child that might have been the child of any one of fourteen youths; which is the first really shocking thing, apart from *London Life*, that has been mentioned. Even the game of Monopoly, very popular hereabouts, we are told—as if it were not popular at the time in a dozen languages—is presented as a sign of a grasping, selfish world without any sense of responsibility for seduced children, early divorces or the ancient soil abused by new bungalows. "You couldn't live," we are told, "in a place like this; it was somewhere to which you returned for sleep and rissoles by the 6.50 or the 7.25."

Obviously, common sense tells us, all this exists, or for hell's sake is made to exist, only in his own lacerated imagination. One sympathises sincerely. The place is evidently associated with some deep, unhealed traumatic wound. But one suspects that when he sets off for the wilds of Mexico (to which this is the Prologue) he will find everything just as squalid and heartless. He does. All he has to do is to change the names and the circumstances: the impression is in the same colour, a general rot-green light. The only important difference is that he implies, not very persuasively, that if the Mexican people were allowed to practise their old religion in complete freedom life there would be less squalid. To which one can only reply that nobody is hunting down Catholics with police-dogs in Hertfordshire. But it would be pointless to argue rationally about all this, since the man is clearly not talking about objective conditions at all. We must agree, however, that it is an achievement to be able to see the devil in unlikely places, for he doubtless is everywhere. Mauriac has not a finer nose for Satan. Pascal had not a finer ear when he heard the voice of Beelzebub among the Jesuits than Greene hearing the authentic whisper of eternal corruption in the chiming door-bell of the Plough Inn and the innocent flick of billiard balls. This is real tin-chapel stuff. Bunyan suffered the same agonies in the Bedford pubs.

We can understand so much without difficulty; but two puzzles suggest themselves. It is good to see evil on many sides if it helps to remind us constantly that good and Godliness are just around the corner. Why, however, must they always be around the corner, never walking down the High Street? It is also good to be able to show, if one persuasively can, that there is no real essential difference between native and foreign forms of evil: that nobody living in the Home Counties has the right to be smugly horrified by the affairs of Chiapas or Tabasco, with priests hiding in swamps and being shot when found there, hotel lavatories ankle-deep in ordure, flies that produce a hideous form of blindness, dead beetles lying on the floor being devoured by long processions of hungry ants, buzzards on tin-roofs, and so forth and so on. But, if wherever one goes – London, Brighton, Mexico, Stockholm, Vienna, Stamboul, Indo-China – one will always find the same story, why stir at all? The answer evokes what may be the essential question: that although it is true that whenever a moralist writes he describes a *voyage autour de son âme*, why does no other moralist bring back such a consistently identical story? Greene must then be some special sort of moralist; whereupon the essential questions arise: What is his sort? What is his tradition?

2

I suggest that the only comparable modern analogy is with Pascal and Jansenism. It is a literary tradition which has exercised a much more far-reaching influence on the course of modern literature than we commonly realise. Essentially its challenge has been felt as a challenge to the humanists to deny, and prove, that there is not an impassable gulf between pleasure and the virtuous life, between the weakness of human nature and its possibilities of greatness, between all that we like to enjoy and most of the things we pretend to admire. In its hey-day it provoked a profound opposition and when Port-Royal fell it might all seem to have been no more than a flash in the pan. But Pascal did not come out of nothing, and when one is discussing the French nature it is still one of the more agreeable problems to ask what in the French nature produced him. Perhaps it is enough to say that the pessimism of Jansenism is endemic in human nature in general. We may think back to Saint Augustine and the Manicheans, to go no further. What is more to our purpose is to observe how persistently it recurs; the power of an appealing literary form—every French writer must have read and admired Pascal—to keep ideas alive; and the historical fact that the rise of Jansenism coincided with the beginnings of the whole modern high-minded disapproval of aristocratic irresponsibility.

I do not suggest that many writers swallow Pascal whole. But he does seem to offer something to a great many types of writer—the ascetically-minded Catholic, the natural sceptic with no interest in religion (La Rochefoucauld was of the type), the soured hedonist, the frustrated romantic, the earnest social

reformer, the topical satirist. The list of candidates for the title
of neo-Pascalians in our time is long: Bernanos, Julian Green,
Mauriac, Céline, Marcel Aymé, Camus, Faulkner, Moravia,
George Orwell, Graham Greene–all of them anti-humanist,
anti-heroic, highly sceptical about man's inherent dignity
which the great humanist tradition took as the corner-stone of
all its beliefs; full of misgivings as to the nature of free-will.

We had here better re-define our terms since Jansenism is
one of those words that has been so loosely used–almost as a
term of common abuse without any precise meaning, like
Pink, or Liberal, or Left, or Romantic–that anybody using it
as a term of literary criticism is under an obligation to say what
precisely he means by it. The word, we will recall, originated
quite simply out of an exchange of ideas between the abbé of
Saint-Cyran and Jansen, Bishop of Ypres, with a view to a
reform within the Catholic Church. The main documents are
Augustinus which is a sort of anthology of relevant Augustiniana
–Saint Augustine being taken as a representative of the more
extreme, though orthodox, view on the doctrine of Grace, which
was the cardinal point involved; various records of the imprint
the doctrine left on the convent of Port-Royal; the writings of
Pascal, especially the *Lettres provinciales*, that highly entertaining
book in which one may watch the fight between the Jansenists
and the Jesuits as close-up as in television; and the continuing
marks of its influence well on into the eighteenth century in
La Rochefoucauld, Racine, Boileau and others.

From these we gather that the central Jansenist doctrine was
that man cannot be saved by his own efforts. Alone he is
helpless. He depends for salvation on the arbitrary, if not
actually capricious gift of Grace which he can neither achieve
of his own efforts nor, if it is granted to him, resist.

I am simplifying a good deal here. One might mention for a
larger view the distinctions made between various kinds of

Grace, such as what Catholic theologians call "sufficient grace";
or the Grace which suffices to enable a man to choose well, and
which will fail only when he deliberately refuses to co-operate.
Jansen denied its existence. To him, if a man failed it was only
because he had not been given enough assistance from his
Creator, which of course means the end of free-will. One might
put this simply by saying that, to Jansen, if a man had been
granted Grace amounting to only fifty-nine volts and if he had to
face a temptation equal to sixty volts, all was up with him; if it
was the other way round, then Beelzebub was helpless. Both
deny free-will. Indeed, logically, the commandments become
impossible of fulfilment within this savage doctrine. One can see
how utterly it deflates human dignity, confidence and self-pride.

The social and historical origins of Jansenism are also relevant.
Its rise coincided with the growing absolutism of Louis XIV,
the corresponding decline of aristocratic power, so resolutely
assailed by Mazarin and Richelieu, and the corresponding rise
of a bourgeoisie antipathetic to the aristocrats' lavish attitude
to life in general. One can understand how Jansenism with its
stress on self-discipline, and prudence and forethought would
appeal to the bourgeois conscience. The strange thing is that
it did not appeal more to the bourgeois sense of moderation.
The princes of the Church, however, did not consider it a
moderate doctrine: they had learned on too many a battlefield
that while it is all very well to remind us that as compared with
our Creator we are brute beasts there is always the danger that
we may take it so much to heart as to act on it. The Church
knew that nothing corrupts like excess. Pascal knows no such
benevolence. He rubs man's face into the mud. "*La grandeur
de l'homme est grande en ce qu'il se connait misérable.*" Even after
he has received the gift of divine Grace he does not alter his
nature–though he may change his object.

The probable effects of such a doctrine on literature seem

evident. What price glory now? It becomes mere self-love. One might even argue that Pascal is a sort of theological fore-runner of egalitarianism; as when in his *Trois Discours sur la Condition des Grands* he rails against the people who think that the great ones of the earth are in any real sense great.[1] Man as Hero could not, evidently, long survive such an attitude. If we are subject to all those weaknesses with which Pascal makes such play, our inconstancy, our self-contradictions, our tempera-ment, our credulity, all our palpitating sensibilities, we are not masters of our fates but slaves of chance, blind instruments of our own vanities. Inevitably, in this dispensation, the Corneillian concept of man as a Hero–to the Jansenists at once absurd and sinful–gave way to Racine and the theme of fated passion. It was to be a hundred years before romantic poetry would restore the Hero under another form, but, concurrently, the psychological novel–through Madame de Lafayette, Benjamin Constant, de Laclos, Stendhal and so on into the nineteenth century–demonstrates and accelerates what Mr Martin Turnell has so well called the "disintegration of personality" begun by the Pascalian way of looking at life. One does not, to be sure, deny that this modern disintegration had other origins.

With so much by way of definition let us now turn back to Greene's novels and observe four of their cardinal characteristics.

3

(1) *The obsessive theme.* It has been said frequently that his obsessive theme is the Hunted Man. This is true only if we take the phrase in the sense of a man hunted by himself: the sense of the epigraph to his first novel *The Man Within*: "There's another man within me that's angry with me." In the literal sense, the hunted man is not the subject of *The End of the Affair,*

[1] In all this I am much indebted to *Morales du Grand Siècle*; by Paul Bénichou. Paris, 1948.

The Heart of the Matter, Brighton Rock (not the subject, though it is a thread in the story), *It's a Battlefield, Stamboul Train* (unless one strains a point to make Czinner the central character), or *Rumour at Nightfall*. He is the subject of *A Gun for Sale* and *The Power and the Glory*. In any case he is never the theme of Greene's novels. His persistent theme is betrayal under one form or another; treason, unfaithfulness, the double-cross, the let-down, the broken trust. This may be why there is such a strong suggestion of a sense of grievance in all his work, a certain sulkiness in his attitude to life which reminds one of Claude-Edmonde Magny's remark about Hemingway, that behind the mask of the hero there is the face of a *pauvre petit garçon*, a little boy whose bun was stolen by somebody when he was very young. Somebody has said that there is no use in playing a game where everybody cheats. Everybody cheats Greene in Greene's world.

Let us test this suggestion that betrayal is his central theme. In *The Man Within* a smuggler betrays his best friend and his fellow-smugglers. In *Rumour at Nightfall* two journalists, Crane and Chase, are attracted to the same woman. Crane betrays Chase to her. Chase then betrays Crane to the authorities. The woman thereupon, having married Crane only a few hours before, takes Chase to her heart. The bitter moral of *Stamboul Train* is that faithfulness never pays. Czinner the idealist revolutionary is shot. The honest little trollop Coral Musker is overnight swopped by the business-man Myatt for the quondam Lesbian, Janet Purdoe, who thereby betrays her former friend Mabel Warren, who now takes on Coral Musker, after being instrumental in bringing about Czinner's death. In *It's a Battle-field*, where everybody lets down everybody else and gets nothing much out of it, the only conclusion open to us is that unfaithfulness does not pay either. Here Jim Drover, a Communist, is under sentence of death. His wife betrays him, his brother betrays him, Condor a journalist betrays his pals, his sister-in-law is unfaithful all round, Surrogate the writer is unfaithful to his dead wife, and the Assistant Commissioner of Police decides in his devotion to the law that he must not be over-loyal to Justice. In *Brighton Rock* the whole central story of Rose and Pinkie turns on betrayal or the fear of betrayal. Pinkie murders Hale for having betrayed the gang, then betrays Spicer, then seduces Rose lest she should betray him. *The Ministry of Fear*, a war story, is specifically concerned with traitors. In *England Made Me* we are in the world of international finance where Kate Farrant is the only really reliable character: the central figure, Tony Farrant, might truthfully be described as the sort of charm-dispensing liar who would double-cross his sister, since that is precisely what he does. In *A Gun for Sale* the hare-lipped assassin is double-crossed by his employers, and any pity we may feel for this murderous maniac comes from his vain hope that Anne, the detective's girl, will not give him away to the police, which she has to do. In *The Heart of the Matter* Scobie is unfaithful to his wife, lets his mistress down, and his servant, and one may fairly hold the view that his final gamble for salvation is on the border-line of a double-cross on God. But we are given to understand that God is treated poorly by most of the characters in these stories. Raven, seeing the infant Christ in the Crib, thinks: There He lies waiting "for the double-cross, the whip, the nails". This general unfaithfulness is symbolical of mankind's eternally renewed Judas kiss.

(2) *The denial of free-will*. All these characters, we are made to feel, are coping with circumstances beyond their power. The dice is loaded against them. They are fissurated by self-interest, self-distrust, self-pity, ambition, lust, greed, fear, hate, weak longing for peace at any price, and, most dissolvent weakness of all, human respect. They are, indeed, permitted to have glimpses of the Good Life, but the battle that takes place within

their conscience—where the act of treason takes place—is a
foregone conclusion. It is true that when we first come to these
grim novels we have hopes that somebody will rise superior to
the brute. Once we have become familiar with the obsessive
theme we know that these brief spurts of gallantry will soon
die. For example, one might, if one did not know the line of fate
as Greene sees it, have, for a while, high hopes that Myatt, in
Stamboul Train, will delight us by sticking pluckily to the
chorus-girl, Coral. And Greene tries hard to be fair to Myatt,
or seems to be trying, though since Myatt like everybody else
in the novel except Czinner collapses in the end, one cannot
avoid feeling that Greene has given only that he may in the end
take away. Or we might hope that Conrad Drover in *It's a
Battlefield* will at least succeed in shooting the Police Commissioner. Knowing the fore-ordained line of fate we are
sardonically gratified when he merely succeeds in shooting at
the Commissioner with blank cartridges. Nobody in Greene's
novels stands a dog's chance.

Greene was not always so hopeless of humanity. He had a
romantic period at the start of his career represented by three
novels of which he has since suppressed two. In this period his
men were, to be sure, just as prone to evil, but he did allow to
some of them gestures of real self-perception, self-truth and
final regeneration. I think he may still have hoped at this period
that man could save himself. There is a curious passage in
Rumour at Nightfall which suggests that if he could then see this
hope for man it was because he was still seeing life as a conflict
of a purely human order. Crane has found out that his beloved
Eulalia had previously been the lover of a Spaniard. The discovery pains him, but he nourishes this pain in the belief that
without pain Truth is of an inferior quality. In pain one discovers
oneself. Descartes's "I think, therefore I am" becomes "I suffer,
therefore I am." Crane expresses this by calling painless Truth

"comfortable", whereas those who suffer when they see the Truth will not be comfortable, will desire virtue and admiration and courage, even though they may actually in their weakness choose "lies, evasions, compromises, fears and humanity". So Crane by honestly recognising his own cowardice and suffering achieves a final act of courage.

It would be interesting to know what happened in Graham Greene's mind around 1931; for in that year the romantic-humanist period closed with a bang, as if something that had been gnawing at the foundations of his belief in man's power of self-purification brought down the wall separating him from an almost total despair of human nature. In that year he wrote *Stamboul Train*, and after that the road is clear. The romantic style vanishes. Decorous expression, reticence, the note of human idealism give way, with those nineteenth-century smugglers and Carlists, to the modern scene painted with all that ruthless brutality, brassiness, brilliance, cruelty, sexiness, tartness, satire and so on which he would finally justify so magnificently in *The Power and the Glory*–though, as we shall note, with the new addition of a mystical escape into final optimism.

It is interesting, possibly revealing, that only two types are permitted to engage our sympathy from *Stamboul Train* onward: priests and trollops. Each of these is outside the battle: the priest because he is sold to heaven, the trollop because she is at least undeceived, knows that she is what she is–Greene loathes all forms of pretence, fake, sentimentality, as the surest paths to the Judas kiss–and, knowing herself, may one day re-enter the battle. See also *The End of the Affair*.

Why does Greene load the dice so completely against his characters? It is the old Jansenist reason that man, of himself, can do nothing. Only God can do it. He was already groping towards this idea in his early romantic period. There, in *Rumour at Nightfall*, we come on the frightening observation that "if

Judas betrayed God, God betrayed Judas by waiting for his
coming". Sin appears to be coercive. People are so caught in
the net that even when they would do good they do harm—it is
the theme of *The Quiet American*—and if they are godless must
do harm: as when Ida in *Brighton Rock* by her pity for Hale
starts a chain of circumstances that brings disaster all round,
or when Rose by her human pity for Pinkie drives him still
deeper into evil. In *Brighton Rock* he allows us at least the chance
of godly help, but it is only a chance, and it remains only a
chance thereafter—if it is permissible to think of a last-minute
miracle as a chance. Pinkie's only hope is expressed in the far
from hopeful verse: "Between the stirrup and the ground he
mercy sought—and mercy found." Scobie's gamble in *The
Heart of the Matter* seems like a million-to-one chance. He
cannot stop desiring Helen; his wife insists on his receiving
Communion; his priest can give him no loop-hole; rather than
go on offending God he kills himself. His only hope is that God
will forgive self-murder because it was done through love of
God.

I confess that when I first read, and reviewed, this novel
I complained that the situation was rigged. Greene had manipulated his character into a neurotic state of mind, with a neurotic
wife, in a corner of Africa, in a corner of his conscience, with a
far from intelligent priest, so that there should be no escape from
his problem but suicide. I should add here, for the benefit of
non-Catholics, that an intelligent priest should have pointed
out his true duty to Scobie: that is, to promise to amend his
life and thereafter to go on struggling against the attractions
of the flesh. For Scobie to reply that he *knew* that he could not
defeat his desires would have been beside the point. Every man
in Scobie's position must try endlessly, hoping for the power he
momentarily lacks. He could be quite sincere in his efforts,
and no priest, however grieved, could refuse him absolution as

long as he was honestly trying. Scobie's refusal to go on trying
was, in Catholic theology, a denial of God's willingness to
co-operate on the battlefield totally at contrast with his final
hope that God would co-operate in mercifulness beyond the
battlefield. Anyway–though this would seem cynical to
Greene's and Scobie's unbending and pride-full conscience–if
Scobie had to commit any lethal act, why, I asked myself,
did Scobie not poison his wife instead of poisoning himself?
He could then have married Helen and spent the rest of his life
in penance. It would certainly be a frightful deed, and a frightful
gamble with salvation, but is murder worse than self-murder?
He cherished his wife too dearly? He did not cherish her so
dearly as to be faithful to her. And a man is bound to cherish
himself just as much as his wife. I now see, however, that
Greene was logical and I was not. He did not rig the story as a
matter of technique; he rigged it as a matter of principle.
Everything he writes is rigged to demonstrate that human
nature is rigged against itself. Besides, and this above all,
Greene is not in the least interested in finding interim or human
solutions to any problem that he poses. He wants situations in
which (symbolically) there can be no solutions of a purely
human nature.

His play *The Living Room* is a very good example of this
rigging on principle. Here a Catholic girl becomes the mistress
of an atheist. She is made to live in a house–a world–where
every room but one is symbolically sealed-off. In this room she
lives, through the play, with two unsympathetic guardians,
both very old women, one of them half-dotty, and a paralysed
priest chained to a bath-chair, whose arguments with the
atheist would be unworthy of the rawest seminarian: this in a
city not ill-supplied with priests of a high intellectual calibre
and capable of giving an influential sympathy to any girl in
such a situation. All the harassed girl can do, we are asked to

accept, is to commit suicide (like Scobie) and at the last second say a prayer remembered from her nursery days. I recall that I left the theatre on the first night in a state of rage which, I later recognised, must have been somewhat like the state of irritation into which the seventeenth-century Jansenists threw their Jesuit opponents—men with a sweeter conception of God's world. And, after all, though Jansen did not allow that man has the power, of himself, to choose between good and evil (*libertas contradictionis*) he did at least allow that man is free from external coercion (*libertas coactione*). Greene seems to me to deny this. The weakness of his method of rigging-on-principle is that it coerces man into sin.

(3) *His belittlement of human nature.* It inevitably follows that Greene tends to reduce man's stature and all his works. It must be unnecessary to give illustrations. I must again insist, however, that we have no right to complain about this. A writer, given a certain *manière de voir*, can only do with it what he can. But we are entitled, and obliged, to consider the resultant technical and moral coercions.

One of these is that Greene by deliberately reducing man's stature, and impugning his free-will, for the purposes of his theme, must always be in grave danger of making his people so subservient to his theme that they become its puppets. It must be left to each reader of *Brighton Rock*, for example, to say whether Pinkie strikes them as a human being or as a puppet. I find him entirely unpersuasive except as something strayed out of a mental home. I suggest that the same is true of Raven in *A Gun for Sale*. Everybody in *It's a Battlefield* with the exception of the boy Jules is coerced to play a fore-ordained role. So are the main characters in *England Made Me*: they are credible only as examples of that form of semi-pathological egotism so neatly intimated by the epigraph from Walt Disney, "All the world owes *me* a living." They are all, like Scobie, vehicles of a preconceived idea. In so far as they come alive they come alive *after* they have been conceived as symbols.

We are forced again and again to the conclusion that Greene is not primarily interested in human beings, human problems, life in general as it is generally lived; that what he is writing is not so much novels as modern Miracle Plays. It is one of his great achievements that so many people can nevertheless read his novels on the naturalistic level, and be persuaded by them on that level; for he has enormous invention, a graphic eye, one of the quickest minds working in fiction today, and an inflammable and infectious imagination. I can only say that I do not believe that he is interested in the matter of his novels one-tenth as much as in their message. In fact I go so far as to doubt if he is in the least interested in human nature except in so far as he can put it into some weird-looking cabinet, saw it up in bits, stick swords into it, fire shots at it, draw the curtain and show us that it has suddenly been transmogrified magically, or miraculously if one prefers, into an angel.

One constant coercion that follows from his treatment of mankind is that their power of intelligent thought is gravely impaired: that faculty which lifts us above the limitations of our natures and our circumstances. Nearly all his people are forced therefore to act violently, and to come to disaster. His people feel rather than think. In this he reminds me of Faulkner whose people are so dominated by an overpowering weight of fate from the past that they can only struggle wildly, violently, and disastrously. It was not so much Greene who began to write thrillers in 1931 as his characters, who ran away with him.

(4) *The mystical escape from nature.* There is a second watershed in Greene's career, after 1931. It occurred somewhere around 1938 when, in *Brighton Rock*, he had taken the ordinary thriller

technique to the limit. Around that year he became involved
by an act of God or Chance in a libel action concerning Miss
Shirley Temple, then a child actress. While acting as film critic
for a humorous paper called *Night and Day*, most unfortunately
for himself but fortunately for literature, he chose to intimate
that Miss Temple was not so much the darling of her coevals
as the *femme fatale* of elderly gentlemen gone a little beyond their
sexual prime. Mr Greene retired to Mexico, wrote *The Lawless
Roads*, and found the theme of *The Power and the Glory*.

It is interesting that the first of these books, a factual record,
was extremely dull, and the second, a play of imagination on
fact, was to prove one of the finest novels of our time in any
language. He saw there that far from being a pessimist in his
sensitiveness to the omnipresence of evil he had all along been a
supreme optimist. He had tortured himself unnecessarily with
the squalor of the world's underground annexes—the furtive
love-making in suburban back-lanes, or under mud-spattered
iron bridges in the shadow of sweet evil-smelling gasometers,
the savageries of race-course gangs, the painted Madam, the
exhausted whore, the cigarette-butt disintegrating in the
lavatory bowl, the dead gangster in his coffin at a peep-show,
the smutty postcard passed around under school desks, all the
tawdry viciousness of which not merely the scum of humanity
but each one of us, but for the grace of God, is capable. He saw
that what he must do with all this was to magnify it more and
more until it exploded, and there at the centre of the foul
explosion would shine the unsullied face of God. Everything
for the best in the worst possible world. So, the priest in *The
Power and the Glory* when dogged by the Judas of the book and
forced to listen to his sordid confession, thinks:

"Man was so limited; he hadn't even the ingenuity to invent a new
vice: the animals knew as much. It was for this world that Christ died:
the more evil you saw and heard about you, the greater glory lay

around the death; it was too easy to die for what was good and beautiful, for home or children or civilisation—it needed a God to die for the
half-hearted and corrupt."

Indeed, the corruption of mankind is a sort of back-handed
tribute to God; it is even a form of godliness to be corrupt; or
at least to be corrupt does not deprive us of a form of godliness,
as the priest argues in a striking and daring passage in which he
looks down at the dirty, yellow-fanged, half-caste traitor
jogging on a mule at his side, and realises the implications of the
Christian belief that man is made after God's image and likeness:

"But at the centre of his own faith there always stood the convincing
mystery—that we are made in God's image—God was the parent,
but He was also the policeman, the criminal, the priest, the maniac
and the judge. Something resembling God dangled from the gibbet
or went into odd attitudes before the bullets in a prison yard or
contorted itself like a camel in the attitude of sex. He would sit in the
confessional and hear the complicated dirty ingenuities which God's
image had thought out: and God's image shook now, up and down
on the mule's back, with the yellow teeth sticking out over the
lower lip. . . . He pressed his hand with a kind of driven tenderness
on the shoulders of God's image."

It is superbly irrational. It is even illogical. Because a maniac
is made in God's image that does not make God a maniac.
Since God has no body it would be anthropomorphic to suggest
that his image is bodily. The essence of man's likeness to God is
intellectual and spiritual, so that a maniac or a fornicator ceases
to act in God's "image" by his behaviour. But such a daring
and finely imaginative passage is not to be shredded to pieces.
It is a sort of poem. It is not to be thought about. It is to be felt
with. To be rational about such things is to be either vulgar or
satirical. Mr Evelyn Waugh could invent a delightful character
who had read too much Graham Greene and ended up as some
sort of specially obscene heretic.

All Graham Greene's best work can only be read as "a sort

of poem", an exciting blend of realism as to its detail and
poetry as to its conception. It is not only the brainless and
predestined quality of his characters that makes them move so
fast: they have been conceived under the emotional pressure of
poetic inspiration which flies them as high as maddened kites.
In this sense, Greene's characters really are hunted men.
The hound of heaven at their heels. It is one significant reason
why they are least interesting when they pause. Then they
come down to earth, to common life, and common life is a
range of experience beyond Greene's powers, since it is outside
his interest.

In *The Power and the Glory*, it will be remembered, the priest
halts in his flight when, in a moment of weakness, he decides to
dodge his fate. It is the one section of the novel in which he
fails to hold us. The mystical escape from common human
nature has been, so to speak, switched off. When the priest
resumes his journey to his Gethsemane the voltage of the novel
at once comes up again. So, one of the finest scenes in the
novel occurs when he is, while trying to buy wine for the Mass,
arrested as a boot-legger and thrown into jail. That night-scene
in the jail, stinking with moral and bodily ordure, when, in the
foul darkness among criminals, he at last publicly admits that
he is a priest, and they, the lowest of the low, do not betray him,
is one of the finest scenes in all fiction.

In Greene as in much of modern fiction the hero has given
place to the martyr. Greene lives vicariously the broken lives
of the betrayed ones of the earth. We, with whatever degree of
misgiving as to his ideas about betrayal, partake in this general
martyrdom, very much as we do also when we read Faulkner,
or Hemingway, or Aymé, or Joyce, whose heroes are broken
or "betrayed" by a more human sort of enemy than Greene's
Jansenistic invention of Innate Evil. In a strange and deeply
moving sense Greene suffers crucifixion for his characters'

sakes. Not that he can hope to redeem them. Within his philosophy the Redemption of man by Christ is perpetually thwarted
by innate evil. All he can give to us is a final hope, not intense,
far from heartening, that our immortal destiny may be greater
than our mortal deserts; but that we have small hope of release
or even relief from the bondage of sin and the devil here below,
the whole burthen of his work gloomily asserts. Sweetness and
light are hereafter, or not at all. Pascal would have sympathised
with this sad message, however shocked by the author's method
of presentation.

I have not attempted to conceal that, over the years, I have
grown a little weary both of Greene's message and his methods.
If one compares his work with Mauriac's one will see that he
has sacrificed too much to both. All Mauriac's best work keeps
a fine balance between his humanity and his beliefs. He knows
that if his beliefs do not demonstrate themselves in the ordinary
world of ordinary people they cannot demonstrate themselves
persuasively at all. So, the mental and emotional processes of
the husband in *A Knot of Vipers* are purely human processes.
They are recognisable and persuasive in proportion as they are
human and normal processes. His characters are ridden by fierce
passions but they deal with their own passions, succumb to
them or surmount them as apparently fully-rounded human
beings. (In his weaker, later novels, the puppet-master's fingers
are sadly visible.) His work has a corresponding variety. I do
not find this variety in Greene's characters or themes; I find
variety only in his brilliant inventiveness of incident, which
seems to be inexhaustibly fertile. All Greene's novels are as
subject to the tyranny of the last page as a railway train is subject
to its destination. They lack autonomy. In Charles du Bos's
words about a certain type of Catholic novelist, "*il se mue
soi-même en un Deus ex machina*". I think the reason Mauriac
never did this in his best work is that he retained his detachment

towards his own Church, and the only work of Greene's in which I wondered whether Greene might not be capable also of this detachment was that which pleased me least, his play *The Living Room*, where there were suggestions of impatience with Catholics' goodness, and piety, and pat answers. (The title could have a satirical ring if there had been any character in the play strong enough to represent a denunciation of those unco' guid people who virtually smothered the unfortunate heroine to death by their appalling goodness.)

In his latest novel to date, *The Quiet American*, we see this habit of simplifying characters, in order to force them to illustrate a point, carried over to a story about a purely political problem. We are as oppressed as ever by a sense of inevitability. The character of the young American is so close to caricature that nothing but disaster can be expected from his ingenuous zeal; gradually we realise, in dismay, that the author has rigged the story in this way for the purposes of a political pamphlet very much as, earlier, he has rigged his stories to make a philosophical or theological observation. I find this particularly distressing in *The Quiet American*. After all, in the "religious" novels the theme, or point, was a general one. Here the point is particular, local and historical; we are, in fact, on the borders of the historical novel. If we lay the book on one side while reading it to consider what our attitude would be to a novel about the theme of the White Man's Burthen, or the theme of the liberation of the Russian peasant by the Communist revolution, we will further realise that we are here on the borders of the propagandist novel: for this young American is not just any young foreigner anywhere—he is specifically a representative figure in a given place at a given time. If this be a just comment it follows that *The Quiet American* is a novel in the class of *Uncle Tom's Cabin*, and is open to a double form of criticism— literary and factual. Simplification, or caricature, whether favourable or unfavourable, is thereby a double fault. I could not in reading this novel help thinking back several times to *For Whom the Bell Tolls*, in which another American comes to Europe to take part in another war, and on almost every count I found the comparison between Hemingway's theme, indicated by the title and the epigraph–generous, general and humane–and Greene's misanthropy both informative and depressing.

I admit, gratefully and admiringly, that Graham Greene has expanded our view of human nature by his constant insistence on divine pity and divine mercy, and he must, in doing this, have brought courage and consolation to a great number of readers. It is hard to believe that the consolation can outlive the discovery that he has not–outside that triumphant book *The Power and the Glory*–wedded the pity and the mercy to the complexity of our common day. It is discouraging that in this latest novel, where the *deus ex machina* is literally out of a machine, he has so little pity of a purely human nature for human nature. "Thy will be done in heaven as it cannot be on earth" is a prayer, and an attitude, that leaves a novelist and his readers very little breathing space or living room.

WILLIAM FAULKNER

or

More genius than talent

(*Note: Every critic of Faulkner must be aware of the argument put forward by certain of his admirers that he is not a novelist at all but a sort of prose-poet. So Mr Malcolm Cowley writes: "Essentially he is not a novelist . . . he is an epic or bardic-poet in prose. . . ." I have assumed in the following essay that Faulkner is a novelist, and wishes to be considered as a novelist. Nothing I have read by any critic who has tried to see the same writer both as a novelist and as a poet in the same book, or who has tried to defend the alleged blending of the two categories (as certain critics of Virginia Woolf try to do), makes sense. It seems evident to me that what Faulkner has tried to do is to write novels as I have earlier defined a novel: that is, prose narratives dealing with a number of characters whom the author has tried to make both persuasive and interesting, deployed in a manner which he, with his point of view, considers fitting, and which he hopes to induce us to consider fitting also.*

The basic assumption of the Novel—call it what we will, parable, allegory, legend—is that it is dealing with people who are persuasive and interesting as recognisable fellow-beings. When a would-be novelist is described as a bardic-poet he is being absolved from this limitation and is thereby put outside the realm of criticism. In practice, Mr Malcolm Cowley inconsistently treats Faulkner as a novelist within the definition I have given: as do all critics of Virginia Woolf. Mr Cowley's "Essentially he is not a novelist", etc., is merely a way of evading the admission that Faulkner—like Mrs Woolf—all too often tries to evade the inevitable assumptions of this craft, or, for one reason or another, carelessly or wilfully, neglects them.)

Not long ago I said to an intelligent critic of Joyce: "Tell the truth! Do you not sometimes get utterly exasperated by him?" The critic smiled a slow smile and then replied with disarming honesty: "As an *avant-garde* critic I can never afford to be exasperated." I was so impressed by this honest admission that it was not for several days after that I realised how insulting to an author it is not to be occasionally exasperated by him; for one presumes, respectfully, that every author is being sincere, and if an author is sincere he is almost certain to be exasperating at some time or other. It is only the insincere authors who are not exasperating: they are too smart for that. It is therefore a tribute to Faulkner to say that he is probably the most exasperating author who ever deserved our respect.

It is always provoking when a writer has more genius than talent. Sean O'Casey, with whom Faulkner might be compared, is this sort of writer. Gorki was another; so was Whitman. You never know what is going to come out of their mouths, golden wisdom or the most abysmal folly, and they, least of all, know it because one of the great gifts that God gave them is their unself-consciousness. When they are really writing, that is, speaking out of their natural genius, the Holy Ghost talks

through their mouths; when the divine current is not working
they talk through their hats.

We are very familiar with this type of genius in Ireland, and
from what little I have seen of Mississippi and all I have read
about it, life there sounds very much like life in County Cork.
There is the same passionate provincialism, the same local
patriotism; the same southern nationalism – those long explicit
speeches of Gavin Stevens in *Intruder in the Dust* might, *mutatis
mutandis*, be uttered by a southern Irishman; the same feeling
that whatever happens in Ballydehob or in Jefferson has never
happened anywhere else before, and is more important than
anything that happened in any period of history in any part of
the cosmos; there is the same vanity of an old race; the same
gnawing sense of old defeat; the same capacity for intense
hatred; a good deal of the same harsh folk-humour; the same
acidity; the same oscillation between unbounded self-confidence
and total despair; the same escape through sport and drink.
There are, of course, differences. There is, for example, no
escape in Ireland through sex. But there are enough similarities
to make one sympathise profoundly with any writer born into
such a community, and admire any writer who, as Faulkner has
not been, is not silenced by the disadvantages of birth, education
and tradition.

To read Faulkner is to invite a mixed and troubling pleasure.
He is an ingenuous man, of strong feelings, a dedicated sincerity
and poor equipment: a maimed genius. By no means the least
of his handicaps – and from the point of view of mere pleasure
as a Common Reader it is one of his greatest – is the fact that he
cannot write plain English; not because he is untutored but
because his psyche is completely out of his control. In this, again,
he is strongly reminiscent of O'Casey. There are times when he
seems to be writing with a blunt chisel on his grandfather's
grave-stone alone at midnight by candlelight; and times when

he seems to be babbling into a microphone as if he were address-
ing a crowd of twenty thousand people. This creates a strong
and often wholly justifiable temptation in the reader to cease
to pay attention; thereby, it may be, losing some of his best
things when, quite without warning, the divine current is
switched on again. The attentive listener nudges one awake
with, "That was *good!*"; one pricks up one's ears; by the time
one has caught his drift once more the divine current has
probably been switched off again.

Another of his disconcerting ways is his weakness for picking
up the bright tricks of other writers: for example, his wilful,
sporadic use of symbolism or his use of the famous Joyceian
rhythms.[1]

Now, no style, no influence, could be more alien to Faulkner's

---

[1] The Joyceian rhythms are various but for the most part they are based on
what one may call the Reversed Rhythm, of which the simplest example is:
"The melon he had he held against my face." (It is reminiscent of the rhythm
of Latin prose–*Melonem quem habuit contra faciem meam tenuit.* P. 43:
the references are to the Bodley Head edition of *Ulysses*: London, 1937.)
The normal order of subject, verb, object, is reversed or partly reversed.
This, elaborated, gives us the rhythm of (p. 25): "His mother's prostrate body
the fiery Columbanus in holy zeal bestrode"; instead of, "The fiery Columbanus bestrode his mother's prostrate body in fiery zeal." The intention is
to place the emphasis less on the statement than on the visual image. So,
again directing our attention to image rather than action (p. 33): "On his wise
shoulders through the checkerwork of leaves the sun flung spangles, dancing
coins." Or (p. 46): "Weary too in sight of lovers, lascivious men, a naked
woman shining in her courts, she draws a toil of waters." This becomes
infectious, urging a phrase to the foreground and then grudgingly yielding
the verb, as in (p. 35): "Wombed in sin darkness I was too, made not
begotten." (P. 35): "In a Greek watercloset he breathed his last." More
elaborately (p. 40): "Lover for her love he prowled with Colonel Richard
Burke, tanist of his sept, under the walls of Clerkenwell and, crouching, saw
a flame of vengeance hurl them upward in the fog." The normal flow of
sense being broken, the whole movement slows, until this Reversed Rhythm
might be called a Hesitation Waltz: thus (p. 31): "Their eyes knew the years
of wandering and, patient, knew the dishonours of their flesh." The ultimate
so-called stream-of-consciousness style thus becomes an eddying, broken,
halting stream, in slow motion, intellectually controlled, reined-in

nature, which is wild-rushing and torrential as his later books show; so that I feel it rather comical to come upon him shackling himself at the very beginning of his career, in *Soldier's Pay*, by such sentences as these: "Januarius Jones, baggy in grey tweed, being lately a fellow of Latin in a small college, leaned upon a gate of iron grill-work, breaking a levee of green and embryonically starred honeysuckle, watching April busy in a hyacinth dew." Or: "A branch dappled the rector's brow: a laureled Jove." Or: "Jones rose and under his eyes she walked mincing and graceful, theatrical with body-consciousness to the desk." Or: "Sparse old silver on a buffet shadowed heavily under a high fanlight of colored glass, identical with the one above the entrance, her fragile white dress across the table from him: he could imagine her long subtle legs, like Atalanta's reft for running." One could find other instances from *Soldier's Pay* of this Joycean influence.

He was still prone to literary kleptomania in his second novel, as three sentences from *Mosquitoes* show:

"Outside the window New Orleans, the vieux carré, brooded in a faintly tarnished languor like an ageing yet still beautiful courtesan in a smoke-filled room, [*Yellow Book*] avid yet weary too of ardent ways. [*Joyce: Art thou not weary of ardent ways?*] Above the city summer was hushed into the bowled, weary passion of the sky. [*Omar Khayyam?*] Spring and the cruelest months [*Eliot*] were gone. . . ."

firmly. The verb, which as we have seen Joyce demotes in preference to the noun, finally tends either to hide away or vanish altogether or to decline into participles:

"On the steps of the Paris Stock Exchange the gold-skinned men quoting prices on their gemmed finger. Gabbles of geese. They swarmed loud, uncouth about the temple, their heads thickplotting under maladroit silk hats. Not theirs: these clothes, this speech, these gestures. Their full, slow eyes, belied the words, the gestures eager and unoffending, but knew the rancours massed about them and knew their zeal was vain. Vain patience to keep and hoard. Time surely would scatter all. A hoard heaped by the roadside: plundered and passing on. Their eyes knew the years of wandering and, patient, knew the dishonours of their flesh."

In *Pylon*, ten years after his first effort, he is still, as almost any dozen pages will show, writing under these influences. At the same time he is writing like this, from *Soldier's Pay*:

"The trumpets in his blood, the symphony of living, died away. The golden sand of hours bowled by day ran through the narrow neck of time into the corresponding globe of night, to be inverted and so flow back again. Jones felt the slow black sand of time marking his life away. 'Hush,' he said, 'don't spoil it.' The sentries in her blood lay down, but they lay down near the ramparts with the arms in their hands, waiting the alarm, the inevitable stand-to, and they sat clasped in the vaguely gleamed twilight of the room, Jones a fat Mirandola in a chaste Platonic nympholepsy, a religio-sentimental orgy in gray tweed, shaping an insincere, fleeting articulation of damp clay to an old imperishable desire, building himself a papier mâché Virgin. . . ."

Which is the onrushing way he really likes.

Then, there is his habit of writing in a variety of techniques. His first book, apart from the borrowed tricks to which I have referred, was entirely conventional. So is his second book, *Mosquitoes*, but it is quite different in its approach: it is intended to convey the impression that it was written by a sophisticated, urbane observer with a talent for reproducing or inventing brittle conversation. The change from *Mosquitoes* is total. In *Sartoris*, all pretensions to sophistication are dropped; he has become subjective, moody, oppressive, but the technique is the straightforward narrative of the normal historical novel. Then comes the highly self-conscious, intellectually conceived involution and incoherence of *The Sound and the Fury*. There is a direct break from all this in *As I Lay Dying*, which is clear-eyed, satirical, folksy and downright funny–I count it one of his best novels. Only in the excellent Snopes scenes is there any continuity between that fine novel and the facile, sexy thriller called *Sanctuary*. This is followed by the deeply felt and deeply

moving blood-myth of *Light in August*; followed in turn by
the feeble pseudo-myth of *Pylon* whose style is as embarrassing
as it is exhausting. So he goes on, unpredictably. I cannot help
recalling that splendidly vicious horse of Jewel Bundren's in
As I Lay Dying, whom Jewel has to corral by swinging out of
its nostrils, leaping on it like a hawk on the back of a crow,
patting its neck with "short strokes, myriad and caressing", at
the same time "cursing him with an obscene ferocity", dodging
his wild kick that makes a noise like a gunshot, stuffing the hay
down to him from the rack, saying: "Eat. Get the Goddam
stuff out of sight while you get the chance, you pussel-gutted
bastard, you sweet son of a bitch." Not being an *avant-garde*
critic I can safely say that Faulkner's Pegasus has a lot of the
infuriating qualities of this "pussel-gutted" animal.

But if we think him unpredictable we must first assure ourselves that it is really he who encourages expectations that he
does not satisfy and not we who arouse them in ourselves.
Consider, for example, the one major expectation which most
novel readers cherish but which he never did anything to
encourage, and which is capital to a critical assessment of what
he is really hoping to do. Most readers nourish a very natural
desire for the illusion of reality in fiction. Apart from the
naturalism of his two first prentice novels Faulkner never
promised us this illusion, and with rare exceptions he has never
given it to us. There is always, as a matter of course, a con-
siderable element of what we call realism in everything he
writes, since it is impossible for anybody to write a novel
without some element of fidelity to recognisable actualities;
but such actualities are not his main interest, and realism,
contrary to popular belief, is not his main technique.

Take the method of presentation used in his first characteristic
novel: *Sartoris*. The last previous page he had written, the
conclusion of *Soldier's Pay*, flows without a jolt into the first

pages of *Sartoris*. On that page, the parson and Gilligan hear welling from within the Negroes' church "the crooning, submerged passion of the dark race. . . . Then the singing died, fading away along the mooned land inevitable with tomorrow and sweat, with sex and death and damnation; and they turned townward under the moon feeling dust in their shoes." All Faulkner's characters have dust in their shoes from that on. It becomes a sandstorm in *Sartoris*, wherein Orpheus leads us so far underground at the first page that the story at once seems less a flower than a vegetable, or perhaps a fungus. The story, like its hero, young Bayard Sartoris, grows out of a cloud of memories as dusky as the inside of a mausoleum. Bayard comes out of an undefined past, evoking a darker and remoter past, with little promise of a future; and, as it transpires, he has no future except final failure and the release of death. The mood is necrolatrous and not for quite a while does it allow us to see even the bare outlines of the theme.

This word "theme" introduces a secondary critical problem, first raised, unwittingly, by Mr Malcolm Cowley on the publication, in 1946, of his Portable Faulkner. It is sufficiently defined by the common use of the phrase "Yoknapatawpha Saga", as if over the intervening years Faulkner had organised his work into an American *Les Thibault*, a *Chroniques de Pasquier* or a *Forsyte Saga*. By 1946 Faulkner's novels were almost all out of print, and his reputation was not wide. Cowley's selection did a great deal to reawaken interest in Faulkner, but it did so in a special way: by choosing pieces which gave a false unity to Faulkner's work, pieces, that is, exclusively related to Yoknapatawpha County and to its history as a microcosm of the South. A great deal has since been written about this real or legendary county, and about Faulkner's treatment of it, but the fact is that one can read the individual novels without any such sense of total integration. So, when a popular (New

American Library) edition of *Sartoris* tells us that "the spiralling descent of the Sartorises [is] traced in the novel" it is simply not so; any more than that old Colonel Sartoris "dominates" the novel. It would be equally impossible for any reader to as much as get a hint from the novel of a social struggle between the family of Sartoris and Snopes: indeed the Snopes family is only mentioned once in a single paragraph. Likewise it is to read things into the novel to see any decline of traditional values in an alleged contrast between Aunt Jenny and Narcissa Benbow on the basis of Snopes's epistolary pursuit of Narcissa. Indeed, the whole of this part of the story is characteristically hazy, as if Faulkner only half understood what he or his characters are doing. When Snopes steals back his own letters, for instance, and Narcissa cannot remember whether or not she had destroyed them one feels that one is dealing with a woman lost in a dream. Likewise, regarded as a document of Southern life, *Sartoris* is as unsatisfying as a portrait-gallery visited by candlelight. Old Bayard had two sisters: we are told nothing whatever about them except the dates of their births. We can form no least image of Old Bayard's son, John, the father of young Bayard, the central figure of the novel. Virginia Sartoris's husband is a blank. The effect of such blanks, combined with the highly subjective method of presentation throughout, is obfuscatory. We have to read a hundred pages before we learn that young Bayard's wife was a Caroline White, that she died in childbirth in 1918, that the general date of the novel is 1919–1920. It is with some trouble that we fix in our minds the line of descent: John, Bayard, John, Bayard, John (or Johnny), so that it is a relief to find that the last-born Sartoris is not again Bayard but Benbow.

The presentation is equally obtuse. It is what the French call *flou*: like a badly focused film. The central character, young Bayard, who gives his name to the title of the book, is a war-shattered aviator, a counterpart of the blinded and half-aware

aviator of *Soldier's Pay*. The whole novel takes on something of
his murkiness, his mental incoherence, the muzziness of a
disintegrated nature shot to pieces by a sense of failure, guilt,
confusion and incipient despair. He fills the air with dark
intimations of mortality. He evokes repeatedly those abstractions
that become so familiar to us in the later novels that one might
call them Faulkner's boss-words, *doom, doomed immortality,
destiny, immortal doom, fatal, fatality, apotheosis*–"the stark
dissolving apotheosis of his name"–life as an *illusion*, the image
of men as *pawns* of God, or of Circumstance, deprived of a
personal will. Whenever Bayard is about, the mood of nature,
in the full tradition of the pathetic fallacy, blends with his own
moody sense of disintegration. So, when he comes back from
hunting to his wife, wet to the skin, his lips cold on hers, his
eyes bleak and haunted, "the trees gesture their black and
sorrowful branches"; it is the season of "dissolution and death".
When he is wandering in the woods in flight from his daemon,
the baying of the hounds dies into echoes that repeat the sound,
until its source is "lost and the very earth itself might have
found voice, grave and sad, and wild with all regret".

Now, Faulkner did not, I think, in the least intend this effect
of a narcotic. It is clear that he originally planned the novel
with more than adequate attention to actuality and then got
lost in his own subjectivity. Without difficulty we can recon-
struct in some detail the genealogical table of his preliminary
notes, and in future editions of the novel this table might well
be appended to the novel. So far as I have been able to see, at
no point within the novel does this plan contradict itself, though
he does contradict it in a couple of details in later stories. We
notice, too, that the soporific effect is often broken by passages
and touches of the most intimately felt realism. He is always
persuasive and detailed when writing about dogs or hunting
or Negroes. The possum-hunt in the middle of the book,

Bayard's visit to the Negroes' cabin towards the end is photo-
graphically vivid. He can be evocatively observant about very
small things, intimate details of common life; as when we hear
that Old Bayard brings buttermilk in a thermos to the bank
every morning, drinks it at noon and sleeps for an hour after it;
or when we watch his dog regularly following his ritual move-
ments on his return home every afternoon. We feel suddenly
the heat and age of the little town on being told that the gold
lettering on the bank windows is "cracked". In *Light in August*
it is delightful to catch on the wing a reference to the idlers sitting
on the "heel-gnawed" steps of a country store. The dog nosing
in a cupboard has a "barometric tail"; the dusty, hot air is
"insect-rasped"; water adheres "in sliding beads" to two
freshly rinsed glasses; a coming frost will tonight shrink the
water in a pool about "rank bayonets of dead grass in fixed
glassy ripples in the brittle darkness"; on a wet day the mourn-
ful sound of the guns "linger in the streaming air like a spreading
stain"; when the sun is half set behind hedges Bayard rides
"stirrup-deep in cold air". But my point is that these realistic
details, which Turgenev would have admired, are so few that if
Faulkner does not accumulate them it can only be that he is not
really interested in them, or in naturalistic presentation at all.

This comparative indifference to or even aversion for an
actuality of detail which he is so well equipped to observe and
utilise, draws our attention back again, now with a new understanding, to the effect of the novel as a whole: to its subjectivity,
to its vague, self-confused, irresolute characters (the only
character who has a will of her own is Aunt Jenny), its pervasive
sense of all-dominating Fate–on the very last pages he calls
his characters "pawns, shaped too late and to an old, dead
pattern, and of which the Player Himself is a little weary"–until
we realise that this is a writer who is not primarily interested in
human beings for their own sakes. If we agree that a writer

does not coldly select his characters and subjects but is chosen
by them, that they are compulsions of his nature, we cannot
but feel that Faulkner is himself involved in the incoherence,
haziness and irresolution of his characters, that they are reflections
of himself. One begins to tremble for a writer so gravely
handicapped.

I am sensitively aware that this is not the usual view taken of
Faulkner's methods. It is more generally assumed that he writes
as he does because he chooses to write that way. If one were at
any point entirely satisfied that he was getting as close to his own
purpose as he wished to get, this assumption would not be, as
I think it is, an abnegation of the function of criticism. But one
gets no such sense of security from his work: least of all from
his groping style. Those sequences of possible words–"it was
seeking, hunting . . ."; "he had invented, made it . . ."; "He
would never have said this, put it into words himself . . ."–
suggest only a man who does not know what he is about to say.
So does the use of second-thought words: "He did not know
why he had been compelled, or anyway needed, to claim it . . .";
"This, anyway, will, shall, must be invulnerable . . ."; "He kept
the style pure and intact and unchanged and inviolate . . ."; "a
willingness to surrender, relinquish himself . . ." Most disconcerting is his way of saying, "I mean . . .", whose corollary
is that he often does not know what he means. The fustian
language he uses is of the same order and origin. He is a writer
not swimming along on the river of his intention but drowning
in it. So, when he writes about "the gasoline-roar of apotheosis"
he is relying on sound rather than sense. It is a common romantic
habit. Is he using, with care, the artist's meaningful language
or the demagogue's careless, rhetorical and often meaningless
language when he writes of an "unbelievable quantity", or of
an "incredible height"? The sounds of words intoxicate him.
"A thunderous and silent solitude." "The oblivious and

arch-adultress." "The apotheosis of his youth assumed a thousand avatars." I must, however, insist that my purpose here is not to find fault with Faulkner for using this type of English–though I think it tedious, ineffective and, at times, bogus. My point is single–to draw attention to the dissociation from what, for short, we may here call common realities; indicated by this romantic style. It is an outward mark of an inward failure to focus clearly.

Pylon is an outstanding example of lack of focus. The characters in this novel move like shadows through shadows, and this is true not only of the drunks–in whose case it would be understandable–but of all the characters. Now, it was particularly necessary that this should not happen in this book. If a writer is describing a fog he himself must not be fogged; if he is treading his way through a jungle he, at least, must have a map; if he is dealing with extraordinary events he must work doubly hard to make them credible. In all his work I have come on no scene more unpersuasive than the fantastic description of how the pilot Shuman copulates acrobatically with Laverne, in the cockpit of his plane while stunting thousands of feet above a crowd, just before she parachutes.

This regrettable scene could be comic. It is patently being presented as a scene of Great Strength. The sequel is even more extraordinary. When Laverne sails to the ground her clothes are blown away from her naked body. One of the officials goes berserk with lust and chases her. If one's sense of humour were raw enough, or strong enough to see the fun in lust–which is, indeed, at times extravagantly absurd–one might, again, take this scene as a comic scene, or as, at least, intended to be a comic scene; but there is nothing in the style of the whole section to suggest that Faulkner was himself amused. The only comic thing in the section is the fustian grandeur of the English. One is driven to conclude that in these odd pages we are very close to

delirium; and this not because the author has chosen to deal with
moonstruck characters–why should he not do so?–or because
the moonstruck characters seem to have taken possession of the
author and made him their slave, but that Malraux was right
when he said that Faulkner conceives his situations in the void
without thinking of characters at all. He pre-imagines, says
Malraux, *l'écrasement des personnages inconnues.* Here we ask
ourselves: whence does this concept of *écrasement* come? If a
novelist begins not with people, but with situations peopled
only by faceless ghosts, will he be able to hold his grip on
empirical reality? And how can we refer back from his imaginative excitement, coruscating in the stratosphere of an un-
populated void, to any kind of living norm? The fact is that we
often cannot.

The only explanation I can offer for Faulkner's frequent
factual inaccuracies and contradictions, which many critics
have noted but which they have usually dismissed indulgently
without comment, is this same alienation or mental dissociation
from common reality. Of these *The Wild Palms* offers a striking
illustration. (It also fits in neatly with Malraux's idea–expanded
further by Magny in her *L'Age du Roman Americain*–that the
psychological characteristics of Faulkner's personages are
strictly predetermined by the necessities of his mechanical
concept of man. But this is, of course, not peculiar to Faulkner:
it is the common mark of the naturalistic novel, which is always
based on a determinist philosophy.) In *The Wild Palms* the
key incident is a bungled abortion. To quote Mlle Magny,
who has also noted the mechanistic influence: "The character
of the doctor [Harry Wilbourne], of Charlotte [his mistress],
the various circumstances of the life they share are all ordained
by this failure; the elements of their lives and characters have
no other reality, no other function except in so far as they
converge on this inevitable catastrophe." Now, this being so,

it is obvious that the circumstances of the abortion should have
been plotted with extreme care. What happens, we will recall,
is that Harry bungles the abortion of his mistress's child not
through incapacity or through ignorance—he has previously
performed an abortion with complete success—but because,
owing to strong feelings of moral delicacy, certain natural
inhibitions and a proper professional distaste, he keeps on
postponing the operation until it is too late for safety. His
character is well built up on those lines and his indecisiveness is
emphasised. Unfortunately, we find if we correlate the dates
given in the course of the novel that, in fact, Faulkner is so
careless about his mechanism that it is he who bungles.
Wilbourne does not delay the operation more than at most
two weeks beyond two months; and, as we know, abortions
can safely be performed far later than this. All we are left with
as a result of Faulkner's carelessness about the dates is that the
tragedy was an accident: this, obviously, cools off the whole point
of the story. We can only conclude that Faulkner was not
sufficiently interested in the essential realities of the narrative
to give them his full attention. It is the all-over impression his
work leaves on the reader. He lets his imagination run away
with, or from, reality.[1]

[1] The essential sequence of dates in *The Wild Palms* is as follows: While in
Chicago, three weeks after Christmas Harry gets a post in Utah, leaves two
mornings later, and so arrives, we presume, around January 20th. "*They had
been there a month, it was almost March now*" brings us to about February 20th.
Three days later the Buckners leave: before they leave Harry performs a
successful abortion on Mrs Buckner. It is on the night of their departure that
Charlotte conceives, as she duly reveals to Harry later, explaining that it had
been too cold for her to get out of bed again for the douche. This night, the
key-date, must be in or before the last week in February.

Later, at an unspecified date, Charlotte returns home to see her children;
as Harry waits for her in a park he recalls that it was *not five months ago* since
they left Chicago for Utah, which, on referring back, would put this date in
the park somewhere in mid-June. Actually, however, we are told a little
farther on that it is now "*not yet June*". This obliges us to fix the date of the
scene in the park, and of Charlotte's return to her husband's home, after

Were he to hear himself spoken of in these terms he would probably be amused, for he doubtless—it seems plain from his work—thinks himself a realist. In fact he has taken the determinism of the naturalist technique and philosophy to its logical absurdity, which is the kind of splendidly honest folly we might, *a priori*, expect from his intense but fundamentally simple nature. Absolute naturalism cannot, of its determinist nature, present a coherent record of anything except a machine. And this, in effect, is what Sartre has said in the most penetrating thing so far written about Faulkner. His metaphysic of time, Sartre points out, involves the denial of the future in so far as it is a denial of a free present. What we call the present is to Faulkner embedded in *and controlled by* an undefined, indefinable and unending continuum which bears no relation to what we call chronological time. What we call the present and future, all that moves towards the future wilfully, is to him a continuation of timeless Fate. He has, in short, drowned himself and all humanity in timelessness. Human potency is castrated. In our sense nothing ever

May 20th (any earlier it would be only four months since they left Chicago for Utah) and before May 31st: "*not yet June*". During her meeting with her husband Charlotte says the abortion took place "a month ago"; which fixes the date of the bungled abortion as being somewhere between the 20th and the 31st of April. Therefore the abortion was not delayed unduly. Everything in the character of Harry Wilbourne which had been built up on the idea that it had been falls to pieces.

Also, it may be noted that when Charlotte was pleading with Harry to perform the abortion she pointed out to him wildly that in thirteen days four months will have passed. It is not clear what she means by this—either four months since she conceived, or four months after she missed her first menstrual period after conception. In either case we were *there* led to believe that Harry performed the abortion after June 20th. The contradictions are apparent.

I have yet to meet an American student of Faulkner who does not consider *The Wild Palms* a very fine and moving love-story. This should not encourage any reader of these pages to think that Americans are indifferent to actuality in literature: it is, rather, part of the attitude which regards Faulkner not as a novelist but as a sort of lyric poet or myth-maker to whom the greatest degree of "poetic licence" must be allowed. It is the only possible attitude which absolves him from normal criticism.

happens: it merely recurs. He has, whether he knows it or not, thereby killed the human will.

Tied up with all this is Faulkner's concept of memory. It is not a power which orders the past. It is an incoherent thing, more in the nature of a trance-like obsession induced by recurrences. Compare his "memories" with Proust's illuminating "essences". Proust nourished a delicate idealism in his search for mortal immortality, surmounting reality and its inevitable corruption. His search for "lost" time found a refined Being within us which "can only be nourished on the essence of things and finds in them alone its subsistence and delight". He nevertheless fashions his magic out of reality by a perpetual sensibility to all its physical details. Nor does Proust, as Claude-Edmonde Magny points out, deride even that intelligence which is the enemy of the "real impression"—as opposed to the images of what produced it, images which are too visual, too fleshy to be "essences". He says explicitly:

"Certainly we are obliged to relive our particular suffering with the courage of a physician who tries over again upon himself an experiment with a dangerous serum. But we ought to think of it under a general form which enables us to some extent to escape from its control by making all men co-partners in our sorrow, and this is not devoid of a certain gratification. Where life closes round us, intelligence pierces an egress. . . . The intellect does not recognise situations in life which have no issue." (*Des situations fermées de la vie sans issue.*)

He invites us likewise to free ourselves by a similar meditation. Nothing could be farther from the epileptic trances and daemonic possessions of Faulkner in which all reality explodes or evaporates before our unintelligent eyes.

If we accept this Faulknerian antagonism to time and free action a great deal in his work at once becomes clear. Logically he should, as part of the general impotence of humanity, no,

write at all; logically, he should find nothing much worth
writing about. But write he must since he is a writer, and anyway his metaphysic is untenable in practice, and nobody of
larger stature than a jelly-fish could live according to it. What
we are therefore to observe is a man struggling in the meshes
of his own self-created dilemma and finding chiefly three ways
out of his dilemma.

The first escape is to contradict himself by permitting the
occasional upsurgence of Will—all those brave and gallant
Civil War scenes; though we note that his heroes are few, and
mostly fated to destruction and failure. The second and more
logical escape is to see men not as men but as an abstraction or
myth called Man. The third is laughter, and is his best escape
of all.

Certain habits in his writing now become more understandable; especially his general air of incoherence and foggi-
ness—for who, with so nihilistic a view of human life, can be
interested in depicting its actualities in loving detail? We can
understand his love for these familiar boss-words of which,
I suggest, the most illuminating is the word *avatar*, which he
uses over and over again, implying perpetual reincarnation.
We can understand his attraction for idiots, "feebs" and sub-
humans, who represent life without hope, direction or intelligence. So with his escape via brutality; via his obsession with
animal sex, to us base, comic or absurd, to him at once normal
in man, and a crude release for that dammed-up energy which,
in another writer, would express itself in scenes of creative
thought or action; via his use of the castration symbol, the
stallion symbol, the myth of blood and soil; and, at his best,
via his satirical humour.

His first escape from his own logic—contradiction—was
inevitable. Sartre calls him in one place, a lost man; and in
another, a mystic. He is both: *une âme damnée*. For, as Sartre

says: "Mystical ecstasies are our only means of escaping from
the temporal world"—what the Common Reader might call
common reality—"and a mystic is always a man who wants
to forget something: his Self, or more generally, language or
formal representation." But mystics generally deny this life
because of their greater interest in another life. Faulkner does
not apparently share this common mystical hope, and so he is,
indeed, in cursing the only world he knows a loser. Side by side,
for excellence, with Sartre's essay I would put Mr Arthos's
illuminating essay *Faulkner's Ritual and Humour*, an examination of his third form of escape from the closed ring he has
built about himself, the escape of laughter. But before dealing
with this, Mr Arthos makes two very illuminating remarks.
He points out that if we are, as Faulkner feels, cursed, "there
must have been some initial evil, some original deviation from
our nature"; which forcibly reminds me of John Henry
Newman's frightened realisation (a man also very conscious of
evil) that "the whole human race must have been implicated in
some terrible aboriginal calamity": a calamity which he, in the
terminology of Christian mythology, would, of course, call
Original Sin, its horror evaded by the beautiful story of a young
god descending on earth to expiate it. Faulkner, however,
Mr Arthos points out, has no such ontology (he calls it "theology"), and in its absence seems to be conscious that he has
been constructing a pseudo-demonology. This, I think, is very
much what Sartre means by saying that Faulkner being lost,
and knowing it, pushes his logic to the fatal end. It is, I think,
very much what Baudelaire meant when he said in *Les Paradis
Artificiels*: "In sum, man is forbidden under pain of intellectual
suicide [*dechéance et mort*] . . . so to alter his destiny as to substi-
tute for it a fate of another order. Every man who refuses to
accept the conditions of life sells his soul." (*Tout homme qui
n'accepte pas les conditions de la vie vend son âme.*) Sooner or later

this would have to dawn on Faulkner. When it does he must realise that he cannot stick to his early premises. He would have to break out of his own jail.

It is precisely because Faulkner has pushed his philosophy to its logical limits in *The Sound and the Fury* that it is such an interesting—as it is an unique—literary experiment. Let us recall it as a test case.

The novel deals with the Compson family. Caroline Bascomb who dies, somewhat unconventionally, four years after the novel is completed, had married one Jason Compson, equally addicted to rye and to the classics. They have had four children: in order of age, Quentin, born in 1890; Candace, born in 1892; Jason, born, or so one reconstructs, in 1894; and Benjamin, born in 1895, gelded in 1913, committed to the lunatic asylum in 1933 and still living. Candace, a wild girl between the ages of fifteen and seventeen, married when eighteen an Indianian named Sidney Herbert Head, on April 25th, 1910, being then pregnant for two months with a female child, later called Quentin, of doubtful parentage—she may be the daughter of one Gerald Bland or of one Dalton Ames. Candace is cast off by Head in 1911, possibly—no other reason is suggested—because he realises that the child is not his.

All this, however, is painful, and uncertain reconstruction, and some of the dates do not click persuasively. For if the girl Quentin was, as we gather, conceived in February 1910, the child would have been born in November 1910; and though admittedly a seven-month baby, this premature birth was not total evidence of pre-marital infidelity. (Possibly, as usual, Faulkner has not worked it out carefully.) I may say that this girl Quentin's age is given as being seventeen in April 1928, whereas she must actually have been seventeen in November 1927. We are told (in an appendix) that Candace then brought her child home and returned no more. This is also contradicted by the novel, where she returns not once but several times. (Modern Library edition; pages 220, 224, 228.) In any case we are also told in the novel that it was her father who brought the child home (page 215). For a number of years, variously given as seventeen and eighteen, she pays her brother Jason two hundred dollars a month to keep the child, because Jason is not wealthy. He is described in the Appendix as having started his own business at the age of thirty. It has to be noted, however, that he is clearly depicted in the novel as being an employee. Jason's age introduces another factual difficulty. We can fix his birth at 1894. It is a little puzzling that, as Benjy's guardian, he has the boy castrated in 1913, since the guardian was himself then only nineteen! We are told (in the Appendix) that Quentin commits suicide on June 2nd, 1910, though I confess, as a reader of normal vigilance, that if I had not been told so (by the Appendix) I should not have observed it on reading this section of the novel. Such is the family and their story, extracted from some typical Faulknerian contradictions.

We know the peculiar way in which the author unfolds the story. Both of the first two sections are obscure. The first is an interweaving of past and present as seen mainly through the mind of an idiot. The second goes back to a date eighteen years earlier and is seen through the mind of a neurotic on the point of committing suicide. The third comes forward again and enters into objectivity, to show us Uncle Jason and his niece the girl Quentin in conflict. And the events of the fourth section, dated two days later, are partly seen through the eyes of the Negro servants and partly through Jason's. Omitting the Quentin flash-back the sequence of days is the Saturday, then the Friday, then the Sunday of Holy Week.

Any value this treatment could have experimentally would depend on its being willed, consistent and successful. It is none of these three things. Why then did he write his book in this tortured fashion? Having imprisoned himself and his characters in a will-less world where all action is fated, whose occupants, like all "lifers", are limited to thought, memory, routine, perhaps to despair, he had to write strabismally, his refracted vision matching the torture of their frustrating situation. The treatment of the first two sections is logically of that order. But the metaphysic begins to break down in section two. There the ambitious and resolute Jason enters in; and while there is, or may be, a suggestion that nothing he can do about young Quentin will avert fate, are we, when we see him attending to his private affairs, his investments for example, to presume that these also are the toys of fate? In the last section there is a revealing sentence about Jason which seems to intimate that the author cannot hold on any longer to the idea of a will-less humanity. This occurs when Jason, chasing after his sister who has robbed him, pauses to plan his line of action: "He could see the opposed forces of his destiny and his will drawing swiftly together now, toward a junction that would be irrevocable; he became cunning. I can't make a blunder, he told himself. There would be just one right thing, without alternatives: he must do that." It is a sentence which reveals clearly the presence both of ambiguity and strain in the double concept of destiny and autonomy (will).

The Sound and the Fury raises, also, the matter of Faulkner's sporadic and capricious use of symbolism. It is more than a minor irritation. For, unless a writer uses his symbolism consistently, and unless it is clear that a symbolic way of speech is an indispensable part not only of his technique but of his nature, the reader must feel that it may be safely ignored. So, when we first take up *The Sound and the Fury* our attention is naturally attracted to the insistence on the Paschal time, on observing that the first, third and fourth of the four chapters of the book

occur on the Saturday, Friday and Sunday of Holy Week in
the year 1928. But what has happened to the Thursday? Where
there is so much insistence on dates they must, we feel, mean
something. We note that the second chapter is dated June 2nd,
1910. Hopefully we remember that Corpus Christi commemor-
ates the establishment of the Christian Pasch, or Eucharist, and
was transferred in the Middle Ages from the Thursday of Holy
Week to its present position in the liturgical year, two months
after Easter. Hopefully we examine the calendar. Alas, June 2nd,
1910, was not Corpus Christi. The date has no symbolical
significance whatever. Again, since so much happens in Holy
Week, on these three April dates, and since the theme emphasises
a recurrent pattern in the lives of the Compsons, our attention is
naturally arrested when we are explicitly told that Candace
Compson married Sidney Herbert Head on April 25th, 1910,
two months before her big brother Quentin committed
suicide. Again we examine the calendar, reasonably expecting
to find that Faulkner will have selected another Easter date.
But in 1910 Easter did not fall on April 25th. Once more a
pointless date. Or, again, when we go through the Easter
liturgy, so rich in symbol and imagery, we fail to come on any
sign that Faulkner has been there before us, as Joyce would
indubitably have been in a like circumstance. A few such
experiences in chase of these symbolic hares–the Joe *Christmas*
name in *Light in August* is another fair example–not unnaturally
lead us to believe that his use of symbol is entirely capricious,
and probably not so much literary as therapeutic: that is to say,
he has found it a helpful occasional stimulant.

It might be added that some critics at least who have concentrated on Faulkner's alleged symbolism do not inspire any
greater confidence: as when Mr Richard Chase, writing of
Light in August in *The Kenyon Review* in the autumn of 1948,
said:

"The word 'burden' seems to have the same significance for the Southern writers as the pack of the peddler had for Hawthorne and Melville: the 'burden' of one's history or of one's continually self-annihilating humanity. Miss Burden, in *Light in August*, is not the only character in Southern fiction so named."

It is an approach which opens up tempting possibilities: ranging from the symbolic sense of Jason to the phallic possibilities of Hightower or Bunch; nor will the careful student ignore the symbolical significance of the name Chase; nor fail to remember, when Bayard Sartoris kisses Drusilla Hawk in *The Odour of Verbena*, that the German for hawk is *Falke*, which suggests clearly that Faulkner must have had incestuous relations with his own great-grandmother. It is the same Mr Chase who has discovered linear and curvular symbolisms in *Light in August* and a special significance in the fact that Mrs McEachern washes the feet of Joe Christmas; given as a transpicuously clear reference to the fact that Christ washed the feet of the disciples; and that Joe Christmas's women are always trying to feed him, including, of all unlikely women, a waitress. The Common Reader will not be unwise to remember Jowett of Balliol's remark about a certain learned German's critical methods: that such methods obscure rather than illuminate and pile up mountains of chaff when there is no more wheat—and skip lightly over Faulkner's actual or alleged symbolism.

As to the success of the experiment of *The Sound and the Fury*, even if no *avant-garde* critic will admit that as a novel it fails disastrously, I think that even the most *avant* of *avant-garde* critics will have to agree that it is so unreadable, in that complete sense of the word *read* which implies to understand, that it might be safely wagered that nobody on earth ever has read or ever will read the novel except Faulkner himself.

Nevertheless, though not an admirable novel, it is an

admirable performance. Houdini has escaped his bonds. Faulkner should, by all the laws of his attitude to life, have been silenced. He has not been silenced. He has found one of two ways of speaking out, if not very clearly. Either he is saying, "Granted my premise this is the way human beings act in real life"; or he is saying, "I am not describing real life and actual human beings. I am writing an allegory of my own feelings about life, my ideas, myself. I am giving you not a novel but a fantasy with the effect of a parable."

I would define it in this latter way, and I suggest that much, if not most, of Faulkner's work is likewise in the region of fantasy, with or without the effect of parable. This also, I suggest, is how the Common Reader reads him, granting him his premises for the purpose of the argument; that is, granting him what I. A. Richards calls emotional belief as against intellectual assent, very much as we give temporary assent to the premises of a poem about the Last Judgement when we do not believe that there is or will be any such thing as a Last Judgement. The reader is impressed, puts the books away, and thereafter remembers them not as books but as a man. In the words of a popular advertisement for petrol, he says, "That's Faulkner, that was." As if he had seen a falling star.

So much for the bonds of logic and escape from them—however partial and unsatisfactory–through self-contradiction. He could not have gone very far in this way, nor did he try to. We may pass over the sexy *Sanctuary*: escape from silence (*le vertige de la page blanche*) through crude violence is the commonest form of pseudo-liberation. In *Light in August* we find that he has paused to take stock of his problem again, and this time he surmounts it magnificently. He does it by going back behind his anger, misery and consequent nihilism to primal causes expressed in the form of a myth big enough to justify them.

It is true that his first impulse may have been, probably was, in the actual world: that he heard about an old local scandal, or had seen a house on fire, or an old shell of a ruined home deep in weeds, and begun to reconnoitre the lives that lay behind; and the success of the novel is partly due to the fact that if the reader so wishes he may find adequate reward in this reconstruction alone. But if he is a more demanding reader he will find behind the reality, as Faulkner himself did, something much more impressive, what, for short, we call a theme, or that essential of all fiction which is not merely entertainment, a *manière de voir*.

As for the human interest, the scaffolding has here been carefully constructed beforehand, and it can be reconstructed with only a little difficulty. Calvin Burden, a high-spirited, idealistic, Northern abolitionist, settled after the Civil War in the South, has among other children a son Nathaniel, born in 1836. Nat is a wanderer. He marries a Mexican Spanish wife named Joanna in 1852 or 1853, who bears him a son, young Calvin, born in 1854. Both Calvins, grandfather and grandson, are shot by one Colonel Sartoris in 1874. Nathaniel then marries, in 1886, aged fifty, a New Englander, who bears him a daughter, Joanna, in 1888. So much for the past, here fully creative and relevant. This Joanna Burden now lives alone in an old house near Jefferson, doing good among the Negroes. She is an upright, self-sacrificing, devoted humanitarian, at first disliked by her neighbours, but, by the time she has reached forty, accepted as an oddity or an aberrant. She is the pivot of the story. Into her lonely and virtuous life, at the age of forty, there comes a white-skinned mulatto named Joe Christmas, aged thirty, a bastard orphan brought up by a dour couple who had taken him out of the orphanage and adopted him, but treated him so severely that his hand is now turned against all mankind. His mixed blood has, in any case, fissurated him so

terribly since childhood that he hardly knows whether he hates
the whites or the Negroes the more. He carries in his blood the
invisible mark of Cain. He seduces the forty-year-old Joanna,
corrupts her almost to the point of insanity, and finding that
she wants to marry him, reform him and, what is entirely
unbearable, that she wants to make of him a protector of the
Negroes–that is, she would make him the prisoner of his own
black blood–he murders her savagely. He flies, is taken, and
is shot. Out of evil (slavery) cometh good (Joanna). Out of
good cometh evil (Joe Christmas).

As in *The Sound and the Fury*, the critical events of the novel
are all compressed into a short span of time. They occupy less
than a single month: the August of 1931. In that month we
begin to read Joanna Burden's tragic story at its tragic conclusion,
at the moment when Lena Grove, a girl from farther north,
who had been seduced by a worthless fellow named Lucas
Birch and has been travelling southward in search of him,
approaches the town of Jefferson just when Joanna's house is
on fire. (Her murderer had set it on fire the night before.) The
twin story of Joanna Burden and Joe Christmas rises in eddies
like the smoke of that fire, casts its smell and fumes over the
whole countryside, reveals itself bit by bit as smoke reveals its
source in a shifting wind. Two other characters act as the
clearing wind: one Byron Bunch, who befriends Lena, and a
retired parson, Hightower. Both of them are rather shadowy
characters and are possibly invented as two good men to offset
the two bad men of the story. Towards the end two more
characters enter, the Hynses, father and mother of Milly Hynes
the mother of Joe Christmas–old Hynes thirsting melo-
dramatically for the death of Christmas, his wife anxious to
save him. About three weeks after she first appeared on the road
south, Lena Grove has her baby and takes again to the road,
now accompanied by Byron Bunch. So the story closes as it

began. It is, all in all, a finely wrought and well-constructed novel.

We now come to the second or thematic interest. The underlying myth is as old as Genesis, that anthology of primal curses: of Adam, and Cain, and Hagar, and Sodom. The myth which Faulkner chose to express Newman's "aboriginal calamity" was that of Babel, felt not in terms of language but of race or blood. The doom inherent in this fatality of birth makes Negro blood and white blood destroy one another, not merely in terms of South and North, but of a mutual, inescapable, personal, archetypal corruption. Joanna's pity for the Negroes corrupts itself by her lust for the mulatto. The two mingled bloods in the mulatto destroy them both. There can be few scenes in literature so horrible as the collapse of Joanna Burden. The sexual excesses of this good middle-aged woman, running naked through her parson father's house, hiding naked in cupboards for the mulatto to find her, strewing herself under bushes in the dark for him to smell her out, are like the cackle of demons at the futility of all human effort to breed goodness out of an aboriginal evil. Before that central tragedy the many weaknesses in the novel are forgiven: the cardboard figures of Hightower and Byron Bunch, the exaggerated caricatures of McEachern or of Hynes; the whole phantom-like quality of both Joanna and Christmas which increases as the myth becomes more and more insistent. In the shadow of the dark myth which Faulkner has evoked it seems right that men and women should present themselves to us as Breughelesque phantoms and grotesques, as giants and dwarfs, not as human beings of normal experience.

We begin, at last, to see why it is inherent in Faulkner's method that his characters should always be now gigantic, now manikin-size, alternately enlarged and diminished by association with, identification with or subjection to forces greater than themselves.

Here, from *Intruder in the Dust*, in his most barbaric sort of English, is a simple example of man reduced to manikin:

"... his uncle came through the door and drew it after him, the heavy steel plunger crashing into its steel groove with a thick oily sound of irrefutable finality like that ultimate cosmolined doom itself when as his uncle said man's machines had at last effaced and obliterated him from the earth and, purposeless now to themselves with nothing left to destroy, closed the last carborundum-grooved door upon their own progenitorless apotheosis behind one clockless lock responsive only to the last stroke of eternity. ..."

Or here is another example of a human being reduced to insignificance. It occurs farther on, in the same novel. The boy is hoping that he and his companions will do what they have to do in time to help the Negro, Lucas Beauchamp; but even as he hopes he does not dare to articulate the hope—"because thinking it into words even only to himself was like the struck match which doesn't dispel the dark but only exposes its terror, one weak flash and glare revealing for a second the empty roads, the dark and empty land's irrevocable, immitigable negation". The same concept is defined, quite explicitly, in the long Gavin Stevens monologue wherein we are bidden to see each unique man being formed by ◦

"the dirt, the earth, which had bred his bones and those of his fathers for six generations, and which was still shaping him into not just a man but a specific man, not with just a man's passions and aspirations and beliefs but the specific passions and hopes and convictions and ways of thinking and acting of a specific kind and even race ..."

There it seems at first that we are to think of Southern Nationalism as an emotional idea atavistically powerful to mould men into a homogeneous form; as when we are told that "only a few of us know that from homogeneity comes anything of a people or for a people of lasting value ... a national character". But before Stevens concludes his speech the threnody swells into the idea that "man's immortality is in the suffering he has endured, his struggle towards the stars in the stepping-stones of his expiations", and we realise that what Faulkner is creating is a sort of anonymous man, a faceless type of all mankind.

This idea is specifically stated by the boy himself, who says he wishes his deed to be anonymous, unpraised, "wanting nothing except his own one anonymous chance to perform something brave and passionate and austere not just in but into man's enduring chronicle ... to be found worthy to present" (with his people) "one united front to the dark abyss the night. ..." Even more specifically still, Stevens states the same idea when he explains how man becomes mob, which becomes mass, which becomes so large that it becomes man again, capable of pity, capable of longing for "the one serene universal light", through his belief in "more than the divinity of individual man (which we in America have debased into a national religion ...) but in the divinity of his continuity as Man". Man – with, we note, the abstraction of the capital letter. In the light of this it is no wonder that it has been asked whether what Faulkner has written are novels or a series of moralisations, disguised as fiction, about the perpetually embryonic plasma of a never-to-be-born abstraction.

One thing is clear. That Faulkner at any time made a clear decision to accept the simple realities of his countryside and write a saga about them is not true. But he has made that essential adjustment occasionally, sporadically, and whenever he has employed the third and most successful solution of all for his dilemma: whenever, that is, he has looked at life with humour. It is strange that he had not come sooner on this dissolvent of tragedy, for the Negroes had come upon it long

before him. They had been more wise than he, more civilised
in the sense of being more life-clever, better artists even in
their folk-lore and folk-songs. For much of what he has written
is a crude, barbaric howl, and nothing that they created out
of an actual physical misery far greater than his subjective misery
is as barbaric or as crude as much of what he has done. But,
then, the Negroes have something that Faulkner has thrown
away or never had: they really are an integral race, though,
like the Jews, a race without a nation, and they have what he
never had or threw away, a real sense of homogeneity. All that
is best in Faulkner came from his closeness of feeling for the
Negro—such as *Light in August*, or *Intruder in the Dust*. Ishmael
learning from Ishmael. He has written best of all when he had
written like a Negro, in the folk-humorous vein of *As I Lay
Dying*. That novel is written by a slave breaking free with
laughter: bitter, cruel, rank laughter, but much more effective
than his angers and his protestations, because, quite simply, it is
true to common experience. It is the sort of humour, made out
of misfortune, that recalls Figaro's famous answer to Aquaviva's
question as to where he got his philosophy: "*L'habitude du
malheur!*" It is humour learned from misfortune, and conquering
it.

Place has been, in this sense, *the* capital influence on Faulkner
as writer. The Negro's lot has illuminated his concept of Man,
yet at the same time darkened it. So might a young South
African be stirred awake to human values, yet confused and
divided also. This catalyst has produced a change, unchanging
itself, unaffected by him whom it changes: its unchangeability,
its exasperation, its timelessness are overpowering. More; it
signifies frustratingly what it does not adequately symbolise,
the dignity of Man. Those black sign-posts, unreadable, confuse
yet point onward. But the subject is inadequate for humanist
treatment. These characters whose abused humanity appeals to

Faulkner so strongly are less than human because they are abused. He, the white, cannot find enough riches here to satisfy his own needs. He therefore has to inflate his themes. This common reality will not stand prolonged examination on the basis of its common reality. Hence his symbolism, his extravagance, his surges of orgiastic emotionalism. Reality (he feels) fails him, lets him down. His realism is therefore a *faux-réalisme*. It is inflated in its anger and its excitement. It is a form of realism like Zola's, sodden with romanticism and self-pity, expressive chiefly of some unsatisfied hunger, like a sexual hunger. It is at its best a howl of protest, negative in answer to negations, altogether a personal despair and a personal frustration. The frustrated characters are projections of his own defeat.

What attracts one in Faulkner is that he has always been "game". He has felt an urge of passion, of pity, towards, one feels, some ideal that he cannot define. One responds with admiration tinged with an affectionate pity that surmounts one's exasperation at the sort of performance he puts up. It is like watching a boxer who is full of spirit but who has no skill, so that one can hardly bear to watch him being mauled. He is at his best when he is laughing, with a face cut to bits and one eye shut. One knows very well that the fight is uneven and why it is uneven. There is no way, for him, of controlling cause and effect inside the old traditional order of values, and he has not enough intellectual equipment either to express his own ideas while utilising the images of traditional society–as Gide, or Elizabeth Bowen, or Virginia Woolf, or even the rebellious Hemingway have done–or to surmount that traditional structure imaginatively as Lawrence did. Everything he writes is written as an angry, passionate, generous, fumbling, rebellious, bewildered and bewildering man.

I have met no American who has agreed with me on this. Indeed, almost nothing in the foregoing is likely to please

American readers of Faulkner. Some do, I fear, belong to that class of *avant-garde* critics who "cannot afford" to be exasperated by writers of Faulkner's eminence. But most of his readers have no critical reputation to protect or establish. Leaving out of account those who read him for his "sexiness", so far as I have been able to understand his appeal lies in his topical reflection of a widespread bewilderment, his nearness to his readers' own awareness of frustration and anger. They do not mind that he asserts nothing, that he not only reflects chaos but is chaotic himself. On the contrary, they enjoy the spectacle of the man struggling with his own chaos. It is like all-in-wrestling. They do not mind that the world he has been creating in his imagination is a world after the Flood. They like such imaginings provided they are dramatic enough. They are not in the least perturbed that he invokes a concept of tradition which is not the handing on of the wisdom of the generations but the denial of it. On the contrary, if one says: "But to Faulkner all tradition is impotent!" they will reply, "Perhaps it *is*!" They are not put off by his barbarous language. On the contrary, they are prepared to see in it a new Altamira. And they will, in passing, draw our attention to various plausible sources of his style: such as the political rhetoric of the South, the punch-drunk, religious fervour of the Baptist backwoods preacher, the folk-mentality of the South with its love for fantasy and exaggeration, the Negro tradition. And if one asks whether these influences are part of a fructive pattern which he would have been wiser to ignore, one may well be met by the sort of statement Mr Malcolm Cowley makes about the Yoknapatawpha Saga: that "all his books in the saga are part of the same living pattern: it is this pattern *and not the printed volumes in which part of it is recorded* that is Faulkner's real achievement".

It must be evident that all such responses to Faulkner's work are on the farthest periphery of literary criticism, if not quite

outside it. What has, indeed, constantly puzzled–and enter-
tained–me about such attitudes is that they are so often maintained by disciples of an otherwise severely rational-analytical
Higher Criticism. They are, ultimately, expressions of Hope
and Faith: that Faulkner is not only a very fine writer, but an
originator whose progeny will emerge in the generations to
come. They pre-empt criticism and make all analysis irrelevant.

I nevertheless prefer to believe that there are explanations
for Faulkner's outlook and methods which are not beyond
understanding, and I have attempted to offer a few. One last
"explanation" I reserve to this point, since it happened to come
to me from an American–an old, Southern, aristocratic lady
who had sensibly enjoyed reading Faulkner for a very sound
and simple reason. "He writes very well," she said, "for a man
who writes about poor white trash." What she meant by this
was that Faulkner is not really in the oldest Southern tradition
at all, does not know it and does not understand it. The people
he knows are, whether poor white trash or not, people without
intelligence or culture, people with (like himself) comparatively
shallow roots in the South, not people made and marked by the
full force of Southern traditions. He is not, in other words,
writing about a defeated South; he is writing about a wrecked
and corrupted South. The Snopes and their ilk are the only
people he really knows. The true race of Sartoris is outside his
gamut; what he produces as Sartorises are romanticisations.
Not being informed by the finest traditions of the pre-Civil
War South all he has to handle are the shards and broken
scraps of an old, lost, rich and complex life. He reflects most
persuasively the ruin, the despair and the night. Nothing of
so much that was fine and fructive and hopeful emerges. No
wonder "tradition" to him is impotent.

One of the truest things said about him was said by Mr Henry
Nash Smith in that tiny periodical devoted to his work, called

Faulkner Studies:[1] "He seems often to be battling publicly with something deep and hostile within himself which he cannot see or define. It is this struggle which causes readers to turn again to books which repel and attract them almost indistinguishably." With which I put the shrewd remark of one of my American students: that I am unfitted to speak about this man, because my approach to literature is too like that of French critics, through the intelligence, seeking an intelligence—and this man is without an intelligence. He is devoured by a daemon and it is this daemon which is his subject.

I find that I can admire Faulkner better as a man than as a writer; except when he is being a humorous writer. He *has* felt those inescapable urges through pity, and passion, towards ideals that he can vaguely feel but never express. His Nobel Prize Speech, his Commencement Address at Pine Manor College, in Wellesley, were eloquent of this in the nobility of their aspirations combined with the total unintelligibility of their ideas. It is his great spirit that pulls him through, and it is, I think, for his spirit that he is to be most admired. If one is insistent on asking for something more, one will always leave him deeply dissatisfied, as I always do.

[1] Summer 1953, Vol. II, No. 2. "William Faulkner and Reality".

ERNEST HEMINGWAY

or

Men without memories

One of the most revealing things about the fiction of Ernest Hemingway is that – with the exception of a very few short pieces and his one really unsatisfactory novel *To Have and Have Not* – he has so far not written about his life in the United States. In most fiction a writer's youth and atavisms lie close to the surface of his thought. One can nearly always trace back the grown man in his own work to formative impressions and influences in his early life. They may have been no more than a springboard, or something to struggle with and cast off, or something to revert to as to an obsession, but they are always known; he makes them known. Only here and there does one get as much as a hint from Hemingway's novels that he ever had parents, a childhood and a home. This self-bereavement is too unusual not to be significant.

It is true that certain accidents in his life could have occasioned it; such as the fact that he learned his trade as a writer in Europe while stationed in Paris for a Toronto newspaper from 1921 onwards; or that he had his first adult home in Paris, as a husband and a father; or that practically all his literary friendships were formed in Paris; or even that he found plenty to write about in Europe, in his wartime experiences on the Italian front in 1918 when he was a slender youth of nineteen, or during

the Spanish Civil War as a mature man, or in his many
journeys through Europe and the Near East as a working
journalist or sportsman. But such accidents have only a
secondary or diminished power over an artist. The man
who is not an artist will adapt his nature to chance; the
artist adapts chance to his own nature. This may be less evident,
or even less necessary for an artist working in a tradition or
school–though even there it is still to a greater or lesser degree
necessary according to the originality of the artist–but it is
absolutely necessary for the artist who is an individualist. And
Hemingway explicitly insists on individuality in art, saying:
"All art is done only by the individual. The individual is all
you ever have and all schools only serve to classify their members
as failures." He is not, in short, the sort of writer who would
have willingly allowed his aesthetic to be moulded so far as this
by the fall of the dice, and his work clearly shows it. It could
not, for instance, be a mere accident that none of his heroines is
American–unless one counts Gordon's wife or Harry's wife in
To Have and Have Not as heroines. His heroines are all Italian,
English and Spanish, an exclusion of American womanhood
that could be described as an un-American inactivity. (He was
kind enough to Dorothy Bridges in *The Fifth Column* to say
that her name might have been Nostalgia. But Margot
Macomber, and all that Wilson the hunter says about her, makes
up for that momentary lapse.) And while it is true that all his
central male figures are Americans, it is not unfair to say that,
in so far as they are all aspects of himself, they are all reflections
of that primal extirpation. He must either have cut away his
youth deliberately, or been obliged to do so by one of those
seeming compulsions of nature which are indistinguishable
from the satisfaction of personal desire. In either case, since
every writer's aesthetic is formed by the compulsions of his
inmost being, this thing may bring us very close to the core of

his personal temperament, and may ultimately throw light on his attitude to life.

One thing it does make clear. Like Faulkner he is subject to a metaphysic of Time which is his own creation. It is the opposite of Faulkner's for whom the human will is dominated by heredity, so that the present and future are, therefore, devoid of autonomy, and in practice non-existent. (If Faulkner burned incense to any old pagan philosopher he should burn it to Heraclitus.) Hemingway on the contrary, came early to believe, or to make himself believe, that the individual human will is autonomous and absolute. There is nothing Jansenistic about Hemingway, if anything he is at the opposite pole–a Pelagian. But he does believe that the will is so constantly in jeopardy that it can only assert itself *briefly*–in what I call a sort of Captive Now, which thereby becomes a cardinal element in his technique and aesthetic.

We cannot tell exactly when he established his mind in this tactical position. He himself encourages us to put it around 1922, on his return from the Near East and the searing experiences of the war between the Turks and the Greeks, but he did not, so far as I know, articulate it until he began to write *Death in the Afternoon* around 1927. The cardinal passage has often been quoted:

"I had just come from the Near East, [he says, in *Death in the Afternoon*] where the Greeks broke the legs of their baggage and transport animals and drove and shoved them off the quay into the shallow water when they abandoned the City of Smyrna, and I remember saying (to Gertrude Stein) that I did not like the bullfights because of the poor horses.

"I was trying to write then and I found the greatest difficulty, aside from knowing truly what you really felt, rather than what you were supposed to feel, and had been taught to feel, was to put down what really happened in action; what the actual things were which produced the emotions you experienced.

"In writing for a newspaper you told what happened and, with one trick and another, you communicated the emotion aided by the element of timeliness which gives a certain emotion to any account of something that has happened on that day; but the real thing, the sequence of motion and fact which made the emotion and which would be as valid in a year or ten years or, with luck and if you stated it purely enough, always, was beyond me and I was working very hard to try to get it. The only place where you could see life and death, i.e., violent death now the wars were over, was in the bullring and I wanted very much to go to Spain where I could study it. I was trying to learn to write, commencing with the simplest things, and one of the simplest things of all and the most fundamental was violent death. It has none of the complications of death by disease, or so-called natural death, or the death of a friend or someone you have loved or have hated, but it is death nevertheless, one of the subjects that a man may write of. I have read many books in which, when the author tried to convey it, he only produced a blur, and I decided this was either because the author had never seen it clearly or, at the moment of it, he had physically or mentally shut his eyes, as one might do if he saw a child that he could not possibly reach for aid, about to be struck by a train. In such a case I suppose he would probably be justified in shutting his eyes as the mere fact of the child being about to be struck by the train was all that he could convey, the actual striking would be an anti-climax, so that the moment before striking might be as far as he could represent. But in the case of an execution by firing-squad, or a hanging, this is not true, and if these very simple things were to be made permanent, as, say, Goya tried to make them in *Los Desastres de la Guerra*, it could not be done with any shutting of the eyes. I had seen certain things, certain simple things of this sort that I remember, but through taking part in them, or, in other cases, having to write of them immediately after and consequently noting the things I needed for instant recording, I had never been able to study them as a man might, for instance, study the death of his father or the hanging of someone, say, that he did not know and would not have to write of immediately after for the first edition of an afternoon newspaper.

"So I went to Spain to see bullfights. . . ."

He saw about fifteen hundred of these "certain definite actions", close-up to the eye of the camera, compressed in time and space.

He was interested, we note, in three things. The first was that, for the comparatively *concentrated spans of time* during which the fights lasted, he found that he could summon enough strength of mind to observe things calmly and clinically, somewhat like a medical student watching a surgical operation in the illuminated pit of a hospital amphitheatre. The second was that he was able, over many repetitions of the same experience, to accumulate enough honesty to *purge his emotions* of all reactions inherited from prejudice or preconception. Here again, the essence of this discipline was that the total experience had to be submitted to conscious feeling in temporal isolation in order to be washed clean of all previous association. The moment was arrested, captured, taken out of context, and held in suspense. When this was done the pure fact, calmly observed, and the pure disinfected feeling, amounted to "what really happened". The third thing that interested him at the bull-fight was the essential drama being played out by the chief actors : *the fight between Life and Death*. We will return later to this third interest.

The first part of his problem, and his solution of it, are epitomised touchingly and amusingly by his reference to his unsatisfactory experiences as a journalist, and if we are searching for his first inklings that such a problem existed in literature, it may well take us behind 1922 to those days when he was a cub reporter on the ambulance-run for the Kansas City *Star*, a youth in his teens, fiddling eagerly with his pencil in preparation for the "what really happens". He soon found himself, as he afterwards did in Europe, foiled by the pressure of the clock ; forced to play for quick effects by exploiting a mechanical audience reaction, playing, that means, on those very things which in watching the bull-fights later on he was to try so hard to eliminate in himself. For the essence of journalism is that nothing is ever really arrested or isolated in time. On the contrary, the journalist always subserves time to that perishable flux which we call the times. (How well-named all those papers are which call themselves *Il Tempo, Le Temps, The Times*.) The journalist is in this sense literally a time-server, conforming to that vast, ephemeral complex of fleeting conventions, prejudices, inhibitions, evasions and plain lies which every newspaper grandiosely calls its tradition, sometimes even more vaingloriously its policy, and from which no journalist is, or ever can be, free. Even if he is only writing about an automobile crash, his story becomes at once part and parcel of a general evanescence, here today, gone tomorrow. Only the artist can hope to cut himself off from recurrent mortality, and he does it simply by realising that the corollary of time is eternity–the one subject never by any chance mentioned in newspapers. The most striking illustration of this is Proust, seeking always to capture the essence of the moment as if he were a magician able to preserve for ever a drop of dew that falls on the palm of a childish hand.

Hemingway's aesthetic is based, to an exaggerated degree, on this technique of the Captive Now. He records experience with a stop-watch. Click, and his story begins; click, and it is finished. No past; no future; no memory; no consequences, or at least none that promise any lasting effect.

With the exception of *Farewell to Arms*, the time-sheet is of the briefest, as if time were being snatched from Death. *For Whom the Bell Tolls* occupies only sixty-eight hours. *Fiesta* occupies, for its main action, one week. *Across the River and Into the Trees* occupies a single week-end. The old man fights his fight with the sea in about forty-eight hours. *To Have and Have Not* is all over in a couple of days. It is "as though some-thing were hurrying us and we could not lose any time to-gether", Catherine Barkley says. Jordan and Cantwell and Henry all have the same sense of there being no time to lose. What is pressing them all is the old enemy of the Now, the tragic, timeless, eternal element that brings the will into being, that will sooner or later destroy it but, if the will has in the meantime asserted itself, cannot defeat it. So we get those six novels from *Fiesta* to *The Old Man and the Sea*, cut off from the past and leading to no future. Professor Carlos Baker has well said that Hemingway's novels are screened at both ends; pointing out also that with a few notable exceptions all Hemingway's characters are, therefore, oddly rootless. "They seem to come from nowhere, move into the now and here, and depart again for nowhere after the elapsed time of the novels." His characters fight out their battles on a lone peak of time, like an Alpine peak cut across by a cloud, so that those on the top of the mountain do not see and are indifferent to the temperate qualities of life in the valley, with its trains, and ships, and roads, and rivers and lakes leading hither and thither, far and wide, according to time-tables that have as little to do with those remote Alpine dramas as the Alps have to do with those who do not challenge them.

The illustration from style is equally notable. Compare his curt periods with those wandering, parenthetic sentences of Faulkner, long as the endless continuum which he calls "time". As fact begins and ends for Hemingway with its first appearance and its physical conclusion, so do his sentences. So, one of the very first stories he published, "Up in Michigan", begins thus:

"Jim Gilmore came to Horton's Bay from Canada. He bought the blacksmith shop from old man Horton. Jim was short and dark with big moustaches and big hands. He was a good horse-shoer and did not look much like a blacksmith even with his leather apron on. He lived upstairs above the blacksmith's shop and took his meals at A. J. Smith's."

As a rule the sentences are about two lines in length, under twenty words. Now and again when he becomes garrulous we are involved in a sentence of as many as thirty-seven words.

This first book also contained ten poems, of which the first
is a frank declaration of his stylistic method:

> *The mills of the gods grind slowly;*
> *But this mill*
> *Chatters in mechanical staccato.*
> *Ugly short infantry of the mind,*
> *Advancing over difficult terrain,*
> *Make this Corona*
> *Their mitrailleuse.*

It was the style he forged, with the firm hammer-blows of a
village smith, to express his aspect of reality. It is evidently
not a style that would have suited Henry James, or Proust, or
Faulkner, or any man for whom each fact is wrapped in a cocoon
of past associations, suggestions, implications, or traditions,
and in expressing which the eye must lift from the object, and
memory and thought begin to dilate and expand—and language
with them.

We begin to see why Hemingway confiscated his own
youth. We see that he was being entirely faithful to himself
when he blandly made, also in *Death in the Afternoon*, the
startling statement, one of the most startling statements ever
made by a writer, that: "Memory, of course, is never true."[1]
In that one sentence childhood, home, parents, relatives,
inherited wisdom (or unwisdom), all traditions, all atavisms,
the entire testament of the past are, if not dismissed, at least
challenged boldly. And yet he was right—as for himself.

---

[1] He is speaking of criticism and the individual talent, which he considers
the sole talent. "The individual is all you have and all schools only serve to
classify their members as failures." The individual artist "goes beyond what
has been done or known and makes something of his own". But there are
long gaps between these original artists, and critics only remember the old
ones, and see many false ones, and trust only to memory instead of feeling.
He, thereupon, utters the sweeping statement: "Memory, of course, is
never true."

There is an interesting illustration of this in his second book, *In Our Time*, the story called " An Indian Camp ".

In this delicate little story, rich and tender with human feeling, Nick Adam's father, a physician like Hemingway's father, rows over to an Indian settlement to deliver a baby by Caesarian section, using only a jack-knife and nine-foot, tapered gut-leaders. When it is all over and the mother's screams have subsided, the doctor takes a look at the husband who has all the time been lying silent in the bunk above her, his face to the wall. He is dead. Unable to bear his wife's screams he has cut his throat with a razor. As father and son walk back to the boat they talk a bit about what has happened and this is how the story ends:

> "'Is dying hard, Daddy?'
> "'No, I think it's pretty easy, Nick. It all depends.'
> "They were seated in the boat, Nick in the stern, his father rowing. The sun was coming up over the hills. A bass jumped, making a circle in the water. Nick trailed his hand in the water. It felt warm in the sharp chill of the morning.
> "In the early morning, sitting in the stern of the boat, with the father rowing, he felt quite sure that he would die."

The story, while it is tender and moving, and perfectly told, has one fatal weakness. It is not by Hemingway. It is derivative. In writing like that he allowed into the story an element – very slight, a mere flicker, no more than the breath of a Mayfly on a still lake – which is shockingly false to his temperament, and which never again appears in the whole run of his work: the element of self-pity. It is a legitimate and natural way of looking at the shortness of life, but it is not the way of a man for whom, at the time he was writing, the shortness of man's life, so far from being an invitation to pity, is a challenge to courage. It is not an attitude which can be related to his almost obsessional insistence on facing the fact of death in order to assert the autonomy of the will.

We begin to see that he has two possible meanings in mind
in saying that "memory, of course, is never true". The first is
that it is untrue not in a practical or moral sense but in the
craftsman's sense; as when we say that a thing is off the true,
or when we speak of a true balance. It is a professional warning,
not at all unlike what a golf professional means when he tells
us to keep our eye on the ball. Once lift your eye from the
actuality of the moment, he seems to say, and you are distracted, deceived, deflected, lose focus, strike without accuracy,
and the next thing you know you are in the rough of the
sentimental, or the bogus. The implication, of course, is that
after a long apprenticeship to the actuality of the moment you
may stop being a catechumen and begin to apply what you have
learned to a variety of experiences. But this is more than
remembering, since each case is different from what you had
learned. You apply the laboratory experiment under new
conditions. It is what every professional does, whether he is a
plumber or an orthodontist. This can be the only technical
meaning to his use of the word true. Otherwise everything that
Dickens, Daudet, Turgenev, Chekov, Gide—the examples are
endless—wrote about their childhood would be false.

The second meaning I put forward more tentatively, and, if
it represents a part of the thought which impelled the statement,
is much more interesting. It implies that, to him, memory
is much too coarse a sieve to hold the delicate and fearful
intrinsicality of the past. It may be thought that this is much too
tremulous and tender an attitude to attribute to a writer of
Hemingway's texture. It may be held that there is nothing in
the course of his work to justify us in thinking him capable of
such a respectful feeling for that past which he has seemed to
ignore or to dismiss with an almost brutal rejection. Yet what
I am suggesting in this essay is that this very rejection arises
from the fact that there *is* in Hemingway's nature a tenderness

which he normally represses or conceals. The few occasions—as in "An Indian Camp"—when he does release it are revealing precisely because they are few.

We shall never know—or not unless fuller biographical material, such as intimate letters, or the recollections of youthful contemporaries, reveals his secret—why he has this inhibition about the past. Was his home-life particularly painful? Were there domestic scenes that hurt him? (We know that his father subsequently committed suicide.) Has all the son's subsequent life been a way of winning in art what the father lost in life? As one might also say of Joyce. Could it possibly be that he who has made so much of heroism is afraid of tenderness? All we can do is to feel our way behind those suppressions of which he himself has given us a few hints; as in that superb and touching story "Fathers and Sons" in the volume *Winner Take Nothing*.

Here Nick Adams does remember his home, his childhood and his father:

"Like all men with a faculty that surpasses human requirements, his father was very nervous. Then, too, he was sentimental, and, like most sentimental people, he was both cruel and abused. Also he had much bad luck, and it was not all of it his own. He had died in a trap that he had helped only a little to set, and they had all betrayed him in various ways before he died. All sentimental people are betrayed so many times."

Perhaps Hemingway's fear of the past is a form of anti-sentimentality? The pose Nick adopts—the only possible word here is pose—when speaking of his dead father's face is illuminating:

"On the other hand his father had the finest pair of eyes he had ever seen and Nick had loved him very much and for a long time. Now, knowing how it had all been, even remembering the earliest times before things had gone badly was not good remembering. If he wrote it he could get rid of it. He had gotten rid of many things by writing them. But it was still too early for that. There were still too many people. So he decided to think of something else. There was nothing to do about his father and he had thought it all through many times. The handsome job the undertaker had done on his father's face had not blurred in his mind and all the rest of it was quite clear, including the responsibilities. He had complimented the undertaker. The undertaker had been both proud and smugly pleased. But it was not the undertaker that had given him that last face. The undertaker had only made certain dashingly executed repairs of doubtful artistic merit . . ."

The roughness does not ring true. What does ring true is the only half-suppressed feeling.

He makes the Colonel in *Across the River and into the Trees* resist sentiment in a not dissimilar way, when thinking of the one-eyed Arnaldo:

"He only loved people, he thought, who had fought or been mutilated. Other people were fine and you liked them and were good friends; but you only felt true tenderness and love for those who had been there and had received the castigation that everyone receives who goes there long enough. So I'm a sucker for crips, he thought, drinking the unwanted drink. And any son of a bitch who has been hit solidly, as every man will be if he stays, then I love him. Yes, his other, good, side said, you love them. I'd rather not love anyone, the Colonel thought. I'd rather have fun. And fun, his good side said to him, you have no fun when you do not love. All right. I love more than any son of the great bitch alive, the Colonel said, but not aloud."

There are other hints of buried feelings. There is the poem "Along with Youth" in which he remembers, sadly, old, lost things, a stuffed bird, piles of old magazines . . .

> . . . *drawers of boyish letters*
> *And the line of love.*
> *They must have ended somewhere. . . .*

Or the poem beginning "All of the Indians are dead" (reminding us of Nick Adams's first affair with an Objibway girl): the long prairies, the moon rising, the ponies dragging at their pickets, ending movingly with:

> Pull an arrow out:
> If you break it
> The wound closes. ...

(Meaning, I take it, that it is an Indian belief that if you break the arrow that wounded you the wound will close.)

> ... The wound closes.
>   Salt is good too
> And wood ashes.
>   Pounding it throbs in the night—
> (or is it the gonorrhea).

Another roughness which rings false; a dodging away from the brief honest confession that an old wound still "throbs in the night". Is this secret night his other private world that he has so rarely faced in print? The little, sad, derivative final verse in the book seems to say so:

> For we have thought the longer thoughts
>   And gone the shorter way.
> And we have danced to devil's tunes,
>   Shivering home to pray;
> To serve one master in the night,
>   Another in the day.

His third and chief interest in the bull-fight, we remember, was not the bulls, or the matadors, or the technique of the fight, or the crowds, or anything living. It was, he says so himself, violent death: that subject which he describes as "one of the simplest things of all and the most fundamental", and which, at the brief moment of the kill in the arena, gave him a sensation of immortality.

Let us look at two brief descriptions of that moment, noting first that "immortality" seems to mean to Hemingway not, as it means to most of us, an extra-mortal eternity but a form of timelessness transported into mortal life. The clock is stopped. There is death and yet there is no death, change yet no dissolution. The moment held in suspense stops the world of nature. It is not an uncommon fancy with poets. "Helen, make me immortal with a kiss." Death cannot touch me, the patriot thinks proudly even while the axe is being sharpened beneath his window. We will also note that the conflict he describes between Life and Death, Time and Eternity, is not occurring in the ring at all. It is a conflict taking place within Hemingway's imagination. Naturally, it could only take place there since Time is itself a purely imaginative or intellectual concept, which exists as an extra-mental reality only in its physical implications, of which the main one is Change. We see Change and we think Time; as when we see the tobacco-ash floating into the ash-tray, leaves falling, our bodies withering. Actually, to halt Time would be not only to halt Change but to postpone Death and therefore put an end to Life. It is this imaginative experience that Hemingway is describing when he tells us about the sense of suspension he felt when watching the *faena*:

"The *faena* that takes a man out of himself and makes him feel immortal while it is proceeding, that gives him an ecstasy that while it is momentary is as profound as any religious ecstasy; moving all the people in the ring together and increasing in emotional intensity as it proceeds, carrying the bullfighter with it, he playing on the crowd through the bull and being moved as it responds in a growing ecstasy of ordered, formal, passionate, increasing disregard for death that leaves you, when it is over, and the death administered to the animal has made it possible, as empty, as changed, and as sad as any major emotion will leave you."

And again:

"Now the essence of the greatest emotional appeal of bullfighting is the feeling of immortality that the bullfighter feels in the middle of a *faena* and that he gives to the spectators. He is performing a work of art, and he is playing with death, bringing it closer, closer, closer to himself. . . . He gives the feeling of his immortality, and, as you watch it, it becomes yours."

Provided, that is, you also see it as a work of art, provided you also see it imaginatively, and not just as a spectacle of a straight fight between a plain man and a plain bull. But Hemingway is asking us in all his work to see life imaginatively, and when he describes something in life–a fight, a battle, a love-scene, a fisherman playing his fish–it is not really the *thing* which is important, to him or for us, but whatever it is that those things symbolise for him, and for us; or to put it in less pompous and suspect language, whatever it is that these things "mean" to him, or "say" to him about the nature of life in general and especially about man living in this mortal world. The reason he chooses those short moments, and those elemental characters he employs, people who never think in any profound sense of that word–when now and again they try to "think", like Jordan or Colonel Cantwell, the effect is embarrassing–is (I suppose at this date one may add "of course") that these general meanings and sayings of life have clustered in his mind over the years around a hard, clear, simple nuclear admiration for heroism in moments of crisis.

I hope it is now safe for me to write down plainly what I have been leading up to all along: that it would be absurd to develop a criticism of this man's work on naturalistic or realistic lines. Certainly he uses the same shapes and forms of nature, men and women, places and things, that everybody uses who speaks in terms of any art. Certainly it is true that he presents those physical people and things with a graphic, naturalistic power

not often surpassed by any contemporary. It is also true that
many people read him for this graphic presentation alone, and
are therefore sometimes puzzled to see why he should be taken
so seriously as an artist. They have failed to see that although his
shapes and forms are ordinary men and women his true subject,
which is Death and everything in life that conspires with it to
make men weak, and everything fine in man that fights against
it, lifts his men and women, *for their great moment*, as far above
the ordinary as, say, Ibsen in his own way uplifts such super-
ficially ordinary characters as Hedda, or Norah, or the Hilda
of *The Master Builder*.

One can go further. Most novelists deal with character, or
characterisation. Hemingway does not. He may think he does,
but that is irrelevant. What he deals with is personality.
Character is a public, social thing formed almost always by
society. Personality is a private, secret thing formed almost
always by the man and the woman alone. It is a distinction
which has been observed by many people who have written
about the individual and the soul. Yeats made it, saying that
personality is what remains when the dross of outward things
falls away in moments of great tragedy and personality burns
with a pure adamantine flame. Catholic thinkers, like Garrigou
Lagrange and Maritain, have insisted on the same distinction,
pointing out that the modern worship of "individualism" is
often completely false and deluded, since what is worshipped
in the end is a mere digit, a cipher in a bureaucrat's blue-print,
not a personal man; and that all that really matters is this
unique personal thing which makes each soul incapable of
being duplicated. This is why novelists who deal with character
rather than personality seek always for the external indications
and stress them. One is told what politics a man has, what
tobacco he smokes, what dress he favours, what his ideas are,
where he lives. The colour of his hair, his ties, his idiosyncrasies

are exploited. In the end one may see a man as one might know him in the club or on a ship. Writers who are interested in personality despise these trappings. They are thinking so hard about the noumenal flame in the man that they cannot be bothered with the external phenomena. If we examine Hemingway's stories we will find that he never bothers very much about externals of this order. What do we know, in this order, about, say, Nurse Barkley? Or Jordan? Or recall that fine story "The Undefeated", about the all-but-undefeated bull and the all-but-defeated matador? We cannot visualise the matador, tell anything about him except that he is at once half a coward and altogether a hero. Hemingway does not care about anything else pertaining to him. He is concerned only with the essences of people as they reveal themselves—and only as they reveal themselves—in certain testing moments, great and small.

He is not interested in anything that could be called reasonable, or that could be tested by what the world calls common sense. He is after another sort of common sense: that gallant form of common sense which is the acceptance of the facts of danger and death. Otherwise he might seem deliberately, and challengingly, to have chosen the sort of conflicts in which reason has no place. The whole action of *For Whom the Bell Tolls* centres on the blowing-up of a bridge which is to be the hub of an attack that the hero knows will be a tragic fiasco. Pablo, in that novel, might strike anybody accustomed to fighting as the only sensible man in the whole crowd—and he is deliberately pictured as a broken man and a coward. But Hemingway might ask: Has heroism any sense to it beyond the fact that it is heroism just because it has no rational defence—that it is a form of mystical sacrifice? He knows that the behaviour of the unhappy Francis Macomber is quite devoid of our sort of common sense. He forces us to see that the whole point of the old man's fight with the fish is that his gallant struggle is pointless, rationally speaking, since he will return in the end of it all with nothing but a skinned skeleton.

To this we must reply that Hemingway either cheats or is blithely inconsistent. We may recall, for example, the Fascist captain who is killed by Sordo's stratagem on the hill-top. Hemingway, as if he were remembering the fun Bluntschli makes of the heroic ass in *Arms and the Man*, presents this captain to us not as a hero but as a foolhardy fanatic.

This is where his *mystique* of heroism becomes ankle-deep. For we suddenly realise that heroism for Heroism's sake is not quite good enough, and we begin, uneasily, to probe into the nature of Heroism itself. We ask: Is a gangster not also a brave man? In other words we come to the point where we feel that it is impossible for any writer to deal satisfyingly with Heroism without considering values, which means the weighing up of motives, which means the development of an implicit criticism of the forces that produce these motives, which means in the long run that the author has to imply his own norm. Put oneself in the place of that Fascist captain on Sordo's hill-top. He made a personal decision. Why? Pride, vanity, ignorance, loyalty to a political system, hate, weakness disguised as strength, a spirit of self-sacrifice for an ideal? The possible reasons are endless. Hemingway blandly calls his state of mind "exaltation" and denies him the palm he gives to Sordo, chiefly, if not entirely, because he was a bad tactician. It is unsatisfying.

The evident truth, as most of us see it, about heroic deeds is that they are done as a rule for two main reasons: in the name of a system, or an ideal, or a religion, or some other social nexus which the hero chooses to represent; or else for some wholly personal vision. But whether the motivation be public or private we cannot dissociate the action from the impulse.

Otherwise the gangster, the murderer, the pimp, the kidnapper dying bravely would be entitled to call himself a hero. Mrs Cecil Woodham Smith's recent history of the famous Charge of the Light Brigade–which those of us who are in our fifties or sixties will remember chiefly from Tennyson's glorification of the "gallant Six Hundred"–has led many of us to think that Lord Cardigan was simply Bluntschli's heroic ass all over again. If we think otherwise we will do so only by relating the incident to a large network of ideas connected with such matters as military discipline, *esprit de corps*, the way empires are finely built and finely defended–in short, with all those things that come under the head of the word Tradition, and which are entirely rejected or neglected or unconsidered by Hemingway.

A good illustration of the weaknesses and pitfalls of a *mystique* divorced from tradition is *Across the River and into the Trees*. Here, for once, Hemingway most unwisely put himself–through his two main characters, the Colonel and the *Contessina*–into contact with the past. He stepped into one of the oldest, most complicated, and most traditional milieus in the world–the Venetian aristocracy–all the more complicated because in our time it is in its probably final stage of disintegration. He seems instinctively to have seen the dangers since he does not set his story among the villas of the Brenta, does not even touch any of the last few remaining private *palazzi*, but sets it, chiefly, in one of the big modern hotels; thereby refusing to admit that it could possibly have been necessary for Colonel Cantwell to have approached cautiously or deviously, explored patiently the complex procedures of the world he has invaded. We never discover, for example, how this American officer managed to become intimate with a *contessina*, though it could, no doubt, have happened quite easily, by luck or design–on the Lido, in Harry's Bar, at a diplomatic cocktail-party. The reason is plain. If we were to be told how it happened Hemingway would have become involved in explanations of the social and moral conventions of Venice. He would thereby have had to start to think, weigh values, become aware of nuances in the relationship he describes. His colonel would have had to become a character totally different to the thoughtless, typical Hemingway type that he is. What the Colonel does is what Lord Cardigan did, and if the young lady had been a real person and not a rugby player's pipe-dream she should have felt at the end of it all like a flower-bed after a Newfoundland had crashed through it. That she apparently takes it all for granted means that whatever she was she was not a Venetian *contessina*, or else she was a rather special sort of Venetian *contessina*, and this has not been explained to us by the author.

By contrast how much better *The Sun Also Rises* is—I count it as far and away his best novel to date—precisely because here values do arise in the clash between the Left Bank expatriates' modes of life and the traditions represented by the bull-fighter Romero. The theme is not over-stated. It is no more than suggested in the opposition between the vitality and decency and dignity of an old race and the moral disintegration of the new intruders, so that the novel fumes in the memory like a thought that one can sense but not define. The fact that the *mystique* is capable of carrying such suggestions, but rarely does, can only mean that Hemingway is generally content to exploit it in a rather too-simple way. The fact is that he probably knows the limits of his powers, and knows also what he likes to do, which is to use strong, bold colours, like a *fauve* painter. But to have attempted to handle the Venetian story in this fashion was a grave misjudgement on his part.

There is something very American about all this. Americans like to talk about their Puritan origins, or their English forebears, or pay lip-service to the influence of the various Christian churches, but their true avatars were the Red Indians. Somebody called Maupassant a *Huron de génie*. The term fits Hemingway perfectly, and it could be applied equally well to a number of American writers of the so-called tough school–except when they are dealing with women, whose scent at once unmans them. The characters of these writers are all out on a limb of life. They are lone scouts. Hemingway never chose a less apt epigraph than when he attached to *For Whom the Bell Tolls* Donne's "No man is an island, entire of itself . . ." All his men are islands, and he does not, cannot and should not try to write of men who are "a part of the maine".

No book showed this better than *For Whom the Bell Tolls* itself. For here he was writing not about a man but about a people, indeed as time was to show, about a whole world preparing for total war. It was a subject which demanded a consideration of all the traditional pieties that he has deliberately excluded from his work, those ancient, often inexpressible things that give sanctity and dignity to common life. If one compares this novel with that fine Spanish trilogy of Arturo Barea, *The Forge*, *The Clash* and *The Track*, one sees at once that what gives Barea's work so much depth and force is the implicit sense of the multitude of things that were at stake for Spain in the Civil War–friendship and faith, boyhood memories, atavisms old as time. I do not deny for a moment that it could have been possible to have made an American the central figure of a novel involving all those things if Hemingway had, say, enough sense of humour, or enough intimate knowledge of Spanish life to intimate certain inevitable incongruities in Jordan's behaviour. The whole of that sleeping-bag incident, for example, would, so treated, have become not embarrassing but revealing. As it was, Spanish readers of the novel were dumbfounded by the incident, realising that a girl like Maria could not conceivably have yielded so swiftly, above all within that tight society of the cave, to a total stranger. (It was Barea who pointed out that Hemingway was apparently confusing the *mores* of two regions in Spain, transferring the morality of a bull-fighter's moll to a region where a very different set of conventions apply.) So, the novel is magnificent when dealing with scenes of action, in all of which Pilar and Pablo and El Sordo and the guerrillas steal the stage from Jordan, and unsatisfying when Jordan is being made to carry the theme of the national struggle. The result of making him a central figure is that in the end the arc of the story's movement is broken abruptly by his death, wherein he dwindles to a mere speck thrown off the whirling wheel of the Spanish tragedy. We follow the broken arc with unsatisfied eyes, eager to know what happened to the really important people, Pilar, Pablo, Maria and the others. The Captive Now device was sadly inapplicable here, the effort to express in the usual brief space of time, in one corner of the arena, through a man who came from nowhere, had no past, is given no build-up, a theme far larger than so sketchy a character could possibly contain.

I think it is interesting to add, for it is highly revealing of the Americanism of all this, that when I said these things in public lectures in the United States I found that I provoked intense disagreement. My listeners said, in effect, sometimes rather angrily: "Jordan died finely! Is that not enough? What more do you want?" The discussion always took the same course from that point. *Me:* "But a gangster can die finely? Is that not enough?" *They:* "But Jordan was fighting Fascism!" *Me:* "Then why did Soviet critics of the novel say that if Hemingway had been a Communist it would have been a great book?" *They:* "What did the Communists mean by that? Did they want pro-Communist propaganda?" *Me:* "Possibly! Indeed probably! But what they thought they wanted was to know what precisely Jordan's ideas and values were, what made him anti-Fascist, what he hoped to achieve and what he hoped to leave behind." To this the answers were either that Jordan was fighting for Democracy, or that he was fighting for his own soul, or that he left behind him a good example of courage, or that he rehabilitated Maria, but in the main the arguments concentrated on Jordan's personal integrity – and on Democracy. I usually skipped Democracy as being a pathless bog, and tried to narrow the argument to Jordan's personal vision of life. And there we always came to a dead-end, for two reasons: the first being that to most of my listeners, it apparently *is* enough to die bravely, for some generally accepted but unexamined system; and the second and most important reason being that Hemingway has not told us enough about Jordan's mind. The Captive Now device, the stop-watch click, had brought him on the stage with no more than a few scraps or tags from his past, just as it showed him off the stage without intimating what effect, if any, he had had on the lives of those with whom he had so briefly crossed paths.

The Hemingway *mystique* has sometimes been called, in a superficial conversational way, a form of Stoicism. The comparison only serves to expose his shallowness. Indeed, it is to do grave injustice to Hemingway to evoke the complexity and variety of that noble philosophy, with its simultaneous belief in a wise and well-ordaining divinity and its frank acceptance of the facts of pain and practical evil; its concurrent belief in the power of the mind to control and enjoy the urges of the body, to partake in the Epicureans' "beautiful arrangement of things", and to "pass from Nature to Nature's God"; its effective blending of a life of useful activity in service to others with a quasi-Oriental love of contemplation. To invite thoughts of that full and complex *mystique* is only to be obliged to think what an unvarious wash of colour even the best of Hemingway's work has drawn across the landscape of life.

We must not invite such comparisons. Hemingway is not a thoughtful man. He has no evident interest in social, moral or philosophical ideas at all. He is not and never pretended to be an intellectual. He is a man who loves gallant men and gallant animals. He is also a man, and it is this which gives him his real stature also as an artist, who loves the gallant spirit, and he has roved the world in search of that flame of the spirit in men and beasts. To capture that flame, to record the moments in which it burns most brightly, has been his life's design. But to explain to us the origins of such moments, to give us their pedigree, is beyond his power. So, as to the psychological reasons why Francis Macomber did not grow up to be a Jordan, or why Jordan did not grow up to be a Francis Macomber, he has not even the inkling of an idea. How could he, having so early decided to confiscate that element of past Time during which men are made whatever they finally are at the testing-hour.

It might seem that, having said that Hemingway has wisely and shrewdly chosen his ground and his gamut in accordance with his instinct for what he can do and cannot do, I am now complaining that he has not done something quite different. On the contrary, while properly pointing out the limitations of his gamut I am trying to draw attention to the excellence of what he actually has achieved by insisting again that what he has achieved has nothing whatever to do with the naturalism with which he is usually associated, for which he is widely read, and which is the source of his widespread popularity. Properly assessed this man is not a popular writer at all, any more than Graham Greene is a popular writer. To explain what I mean let me quote Thierry Maulnier on the nature of all popular art:

"A great art never becomes popular unless it contains ideas and fatalities on the level of average experience, brings them into play on the epic level of violent or social conflict, illustrates them by

imagery of an elementary nature. The reader responds to a work of
art only in proportion as he finds in it whatever idea he has already
formed of himself, of his own life. For the average man leads a double
life. On the one hand, he is preoccupied by all the minor details of
his daily existence; on the other hand he is pleased by whatever
provides him with an escape from his daily round, such as the sight
of splendid self-sacrifice, finely wrought feelings, great causes of
common interest–military, moral, humanitarian and so forth. To
please the average man art must always represent average destinies,
which need not exclude grandeur or good style. There can, then,
be no such thing as a popular art which is not either realistic, or
epical, or moral."

He goes on, therefore, to say that, by contrast with all this, a
Racine could never have been popular, because he rejected all
local colour and all those accidental trappings of time and place,
which always appeal to the romantic sentiment; not to speak
of his subtlety, his hatred of sentimentality and vulgar sublimity,
his aristocratic insistence on ignoring the representative, social
citizen and on writing only about individuals–in short his
exclusive interest in *l'essence de l'homme et son tragique immuable*.

At first glance both Hemingway and Greene seem to be well
described by Maulnier's opening sentences. But are the destinies
which they describe "on the level of average experience"?
Do we find images of ourselves in the Jordan of *For Whom the
Bell Tolls*, or in the whisky-priest of *The Power and the Glory*?
Perhaps if one were young enough, and romantic enough, one
might wish to live vicariously with Jordan, but I have to confess
that as for myself–and I think the same must be true for anyone
over twenty-five–I could no more identify myself with Jordan
than I could identify myself with the Cid, however deeply I may
sympathise with the idea of Jordan or the idea of the Cid.
Jordan certainly identifies himself with a great cause of common
interest. But does Lieutenant Henry in *A Farewell to Arms*, or
anybody in *The Sun Also Rises*, or the old man fighting the fish,

or Colonel Cantwell, or the smuggler in *To Have and Have Not*, or any single character in the whole run of the short stories?

The things that really please the populace in Hemingway are the "local colour and the accidental trappings of time and place which always appeal to the romantic sentiment". Yet, even here I think the populace is being, in the best possible sense, given a complete illusion. Just as Hemingway's supposedly "natural" conversations are completely artificial (again in the best sense of the word), that is, stylised, non-representational— compare them with a dictaphone recording of any actual conversation to see the difference between reality and art—so the deluded reader may find, on looking into the matter, are the doses of "local colour and accidental trappings". I leave him to test the matter for himself in as thorough a manner as he pleases, but I will here give a few brief examples to illustrate how Hemingway actually treats "local colour":

The Sun Also Rises. Total description of the town of Bayonne:

"Bayonne is a nice town. It is like a very clean Spanish town and it is on a big river. Already, so early in the morning, it was very hot on the bridge across the river."

Total description of the cathedral of Bayonne:

"We went out into the street again and took a look at the cathedral. Cohn made some remark about it being a very good example of something or other, I forget what. It seemed like a nice cathedral, nice and dim, like Spanish churches."

Total description of the Landes country:

"There were wide fire-gaps cut through the pines, and you could look up them like avenues and see wooded hills way off. About seven-thirty we had dinner and watched the country through the open window in the diner. It was all sandy pine country full of heather.

There were little clearings with houses in them, and once in a while we passed a sawmill. It got dark and we could feel the country hot and sandy and dark, and about nine o'clock we got into Bayonne."

A Farewell to Arms. Description of the country between Gorizia and Udine:

". . . I looked at the country. The mulberry trees were bare and the fields were brown. There were wet dead leaves on the road from the rows of bare trees and men were working on the road, tamping stone in the ruts from piles of crushed stone along the side of the road between the trees. We saw the town with a mist over it that cut off the mountains. We crossed the river and I saw that it was running high. It had been raining in the mountains."

These are not "accidental trappings of time and place". They are things that are always true, everywhere. They are generally true, not true in a particular time and place. Always Hemingway seeks for these universal things. Earlier I quoted the end of the story, "An Indian Camp," with its description of the morning on the lake. "The sun was coming up over the hills. A bass jumped, making a circle in the water. Nick trailed his hand in the water. It felt warm in the sharp chill of the morning." That circle made by the bass jumping is the mark of Hemingway's art. He gives us the impression that we are there, at that moment, in that particular place, and yet that it is also a sliver of universal and eternal truth. This is what I have meant by saying that properly assessed he is not a "popular" writer. He is, within his honestly stated limits, and despite the weaknesses and idiosyncrasies that belong to the coarser element of his mind, a writer whose subject is *l'essence de l'homme et son tragique immuable.* I dare to say that Racine would have been shocked by his stories, but that if he were patient enough he would have come to understand and admire what Hemingway is seeking. Zola would not have been in the least shocked by him, and would never have been able to understand what he is seeking. I place Hemingway, in his own modest way, in the great and now almost defunct classical tradition.

By his denial of the past and his concentration on the present (the Captive Now), Hemingway has succeeded in rediscovering in men a greater dignity than, I suspect, he had ever hoped to find in them. This is his achievement, and how few, how very few modern writers have arrived so far! Had he not made this discovery he would have been confined to those graphic short stories and sketches which were his first stunned reactions to his experience of life. He persisted and he discovered. When any man does something like this he has won a great, primal victory within his personality over all the enemies of promise: he has found a way out towards writing; he has conquered the blank page. After that the rest is a matter of a growing skill in the writing, and of an ever-developing personality. I am not sure that Hemingway's personality has gone on developing. If it is to develop further he will now have to face up to the limitations of his central device, get more room to spread, humanise his *mystique* by considering—I choose that word—a greater variety of human problems. To do this he will have to summon up the energies of his soul for the greatest act of courage in his long and gallant struggle—the courage to face that past which he has so far buried away in the cupboard with the old dance programmes, piles of letters and faded photographs, memories hitherto too painful to handle. If he can do this without injury to his great technical gifts as an apparently naturalistic writer his popularity will not suffer. The trouble will be that he may well have to sacrifice something of his pseudo-realism that the populace so loves, and his colonels instead of calling abruptly for another martini at the sight of anything in the nature of an intellectual problem—the martini is Hemingway's magical trap-door—may have to pause and endure the less easy and more troublesome experience of considering more carefully whatever matter may be on hand. His work could thereby (or in some other way which it is his task to invent) become finer, and stronger, and take on much more depth. His popular appeal would be almost certain to decline at once–unless his critics fight for him in a full understanding of his problem as a writer, and as a man.

His place in this series of essays on the writer and the Hero is evident: he is the only modern writer of real distinction for whom the Hero does in some form still live. The price he pays for this is that his Hero is always as near as makes no matter to being brainless, has no past, no traditions and no memories. The traditional Hero who was the personification of some widely accepted norm occurs in Hemingway's work only in terms of the traditions of the Spanish bull-fight, or, as Arturo Barea pointed out apropos of *For Whom the Bell Tolls*, he is borrowed and transferred from those traditions. We may regret this exclusive glorification of brute courage, strength, skill and grace, but I doubt if it is a literary criticism to do so. It sounds much more like the sort of social criticism to which Russian writers might be expected to be submitted in the literary columns of *Pravda*. Yet, if we compare his hirsute heroes who are outside tradition with the thoughtful, sensitive, con-sidering, gallant hero of Evelyn Waugh's last two-volume novel, the entirely traditional and wholly anaemic Guy Crouchback, the moral will uncomfortably appear. A man can in our time be brave and add a cubit of heroism to his height when fighting for himself; if he is fighting for a cause or an idea he can still be brave, but instead of becoming a hero he may end up as a war criminal. The moral of Hemingway is that the only possible Hero of our times is the lone wolf. It is an idea wholly in accord with the spirit of the Twenties which he so well represents.

ELIZABETH BOWEN

or

Romance does not pay

We may doubt reasonably that the novels of Miss Elizabeth Bowen would appeal very much to either William Faulkner or Ernest Hemingway. She has too much awareness of tradition. One may believe that they do give pleasure to Evelyn Waugh, if only for their sub-acid humour, and their civilised atmosphere, and because one hears from behind her civil façade that kind of *farouche* note which one associates with teen-age delinquents about to break prison – that is, leave home. More surprisingly at first glance one knows from reviews and passing references that her work has a certain appeal for Graham Greene. Yet, perhaps he alone could explain to Faulkner and Hemingway that all five have at least one thing in common. None of them is at the centre of gravity of contemporary society.

Elizabeth Bowen is detached by birth from that society she describes. She is an Irishwoman, at least one sea apart from English traditions. She descends from that sturdy and creative sub-race we call the Anglo-Irish. At least a part of her literary loyalties are with that long and honourable pedigree that goes back through Shaw, Joyce, George Moore, Somerville and Ross, Yeats, Wilde, Goldsmith, Sheridan, Burke, Swift and Berkeley to the forced marriage of two races, two islands. Born in 1900, she spent her childhood in County Cork and Dublin.

She has written about her Dublin childhood in that delicate piece of autobiography *Three Winters*. She has written about her ancestral Cork home, a bare, tall, impressive, Italianate, limestone house under those North Cork hills where Spenser lived in exile, in her history of her home, *Bowenscourt*. She now lives there. In her novel *The Last September*, she has recorded with an effective blend of nostalgia and pain life in that part of Ireland and in similar houses, during the troubled revolutionary period of the Twenties. Her latest novel, *A World of Love*, also deals with provincial Irish life. Some of her short stories are set in Ireland. She has also written the history of a famous Dublin hotel, *The Shelbourne*. The rest of her books are set in London, the provinces or on the Continent, though there are also Irish sequences in *The House in Paris* and in *The Heat of the Day*. These Irish scenes show her at the peak of her form: she responds strongly to the native scene. She has come to know English life as an exile with an Irish home, a semi-alien though entirely grateful and happy observer.

The effects of this detachment seem to be mainly two. Malice would naturally be more free, and the play of sentiment more indulgent. It is a nice ambivalence. No English writer can have quite the same liberty. One recalls Henry James's remark in comparing the assertiveness of the French mind with the diffidence of the English that whereas the French always have the courage of their perceptions the English have only the courage of their opinions ("when it befalls that we have opinions"). He meant that it is in the nature of the English tradition to nourish the precious fruits of a national preference for the pragmatic view of life–established social pieties, decorum, respect for others, a love of fair play and good humour and decent reticence; all those normal expansive tendencies which mitigate or abrade personal assertiveness and calm down nervous exasperations with the way things happen to be.

One has to be very cross, like Evelyn Waugh, or very intense in a rather un-English way, like Graham Greene, to let fly. A resident alien like Miss Bowen may also stick in the barb. Shaw revelled in the role of the Irish matador. But it also works the other way round with the imported *Janus bifrons* from Ireland or the United States or the Colonies. Katherine Mansfield, for example, loved England even while she was exasperated by it, as her *Letters* show. Janus may write about the new home with even more indulgence than a native; or write about the old home with more indulgence than if he had remained there.

Miss Bowen is indebted to another influence besides her race and her exile to stiffen her own natural, shrewd intelligence, her own natural integrity as an observer. This is the early influence of Flaubert. And when we recall the romantic-realist conflict within Flaubert we may see another reason for thinking of Elizabeth Bowen as a bifrontine writer. The conflict in her work is, in fact, not dissimilar. She wavers between two methods of approach.

The essence of her way of seeing life is that, like the singer who was supposed to be able to break a champagne glass by singing at it, she exposes the brittleness of romance by soliciting it ruthlessly. Time, for her characters, is very far removed from Faulkner's continuum, or Hemingway's feeling for events enclosed-at-both-ends. It is a brittle moment, snatched from fate. Happiness in her novels is rapt away, shop-lifted, and always dearly paid for. God is the shop-walker who makes her characters pay, and we vulgar citizens, the run-of-the-mill of ordinary people, decent fathers of families, impatient of all youthful aberrations cannot deny His justice.

Happiness may even have to be snatched between the moments. She pursues these golden if elusive hours on behalf of her heroines. So, in *The Last September* Francie Montmorency found that during her honeymoon time had been "loose-textured, had had a shining undertone, happiness glittered between the moments". In *To the North* when Cecilia returns to her flat and looks about her at the unfamiliar-familiar ... "Life here, still not quite her own, kept for those few moments unknown tranquillity." Happiness is thus interleaved in the book of life. It is a bonus, a wad of dollars smuggled through the customs of life. But to go after this happiness too hard is, one is led to feel, to wrench from life something that it can only give arbitrarily like a Fairy Godmother. One is not therefore surprised to discover that there is nothing of the Hemingwayan will in her characters. They may seem wilful; they are, in practice, the passive recipients of fate. All they receive from fate is passion, and this receipt is like a soldier's calling-to-the-colours. Her characters are conscripted by passion into action. Once in action they fight well, but what Arnold said of the Celt may be said of them: they go into battle and they always fall. It is true that they may also and for long have desired passion, but the desire is never so powerful as the impulse of chance. Her characters are all played upon.

There is a short story in her second book, *Ann Lee's*, written before she had published her first novel, which neatly illustrates this fateful element in all her later work. It is called "The Parrot". A young girl, Eleanor Fitch, is a companion to an old lady, Mrs Willesden, in whose life nothing ever happens. One morning Eleanor accidentally lets her old lady's parrot fly away. She pursues the gaudy bird in its wayward flight from garden to garden until it pauses in the garden of a Mr Lennicott, a novelist of doubtful repute according to Mrs Willesden. Palpitating, Eleanor enters the garden of this fabulous person, enters his house, meets him in his dressing-gown, has the great adventure of capturing the multi-coloured bird with his assistance. When Lennicott kindly wishes to detain her, offering her fruit, she refuses. "Nobody had ever reached out for her like that so eagerly; she did not want to go back to that house of shut-out sunshine and great furniture where the parrot was royally carried from room to room on trays, and where she was nothing." Eleanor goes back unscathed to her dull routine, thinking: "How world overlapped with world; visible each from the other, yet never to be one."

Now, I have a profound suspicion of that technique of criticism which elucidates the interior meaning of stories, and the secret meanings of an author's mind, by his unconscious use of symbols, but whether this brilliant and far-faring bird luring a potential Proserpine from garden to garden to the haunts of Pluto is or is not—and I think it is—in the full tradition of Flaubertian symbolism (the blueness of Emma Bovary's dream-curtains suggesting the Virgin; and such-like symbols) one may fairly use this fable as a symbol of one of Miss Bowen's favoured types: the dreaming but recusant girl. Longing but vigilant, troubled by her own eagerness, she will, one fine day, follow the bright bird of her dreams into the woods of life and suffer the fate of Proserpine, or worse. There is an atmosphere of ancient fable behind all of Miss Bowen's fiction. Her persons are recognisable temperaments rather than composed characters. Flaubert merely overlays the fabulous. Her characters are the modern, sophisticated, naturalistic novelist's versions of primitive urges. One feels that if she had lived three hundred and fifty years ago when passions rode freely and fiercely she would have described the dreams that drove Ophelia, Juliet and Desdemona to love and to death.

She conveys in a variety of ways this idea that it was all arranged long ago, this idea of fate playing upon her people. For one thing, her style matches her idea. Here is the opening page from *The Last September*. We note how the words and phrases used suggest that everything here is subject to some other agency:

"About six o'clock the sound of a motor, collected out of the wide country and narrowed under the trees of the avenue, brought the household out in excitement on to the steps. Up among the beeches a thin iron gate twanged; the car slid from a net of shadow down the slope to the house. Behind the flashing wind-screen Mr and Mrs Montmorency produced–arms waving and a wild escape to the wind of her motor-veil–an agitation of greeting. They were long-promised visitors. They exclaimed, Sir Richard and Lady Naylor exclaimed and signalled: no one spoke yet. It was a moment of happiness, of perfection."

The moment is perfectly fashioned, carefully observed, the thin twang of the gate, the sun on the wind-screen, the period-fixing veil; but we note that we get, throughout, the sensation, are meant to get the sensation of being exterior spectators, unfused with the characters, not vicariously doing anything. And how little is actively done! The car does not make noise: its noise is "collected . . . narrowed". The arriving guests do not greet the people on the steps: they have "produced an agitation of greeting". Mrs Montmorency does not wave her veil: it escapes. The hosts do not come out on the steps: they are "brought out". The car does not drive down to the house: it slides down, as if out of gear. We get an odd sensation that something is missing, as if the sound-track of a film had gone dead. ("No one spoke yet.") What is missing is the active will, and this has been deliberately cut off, or as deliberately as any author dominated by her personal way of seeing life can do anything deliberately.

The second paragraph of this opening page makes it clear that the sense of outer forces at work has been conveyed as an essential part of the theme. The heroine, Lois, appears on the steps. We have already met this girl in "The Parrot". She is one of Miss Bowen's most rewarding types: the girl emerging, awkwardly for herself and for others, into womanhood, dreaming of romance, seeing herself in a role, troubled by a sort of passionate virginity, equally thirsty for "life" and inadequately wary of its complexities.

"She knew how fresh she must look, like other young girls, and clasping her elbows tightly behind her back tried hard to conceal her embarrassment. The dogs came pattering out from the hall and stood beside her; above, the vast façade of the house stared coldly over the mounting lawns. She wished she could freeze the moment and keep it always. But as the car approached, as it stopped, she stooped down and patted the dogs."

Again, how excellently suggestive! She wished she could freeze the moment, but she suddenly rejects it; and as she does so, stooping down, overcome by reserve, the vast cold façade of the house, staring over the lawn, suggests the impersonal power of a presiding deity. The house, as soon begins to appear, is a clear symbol. It is a predominant agent affecting all those people, but pre-eminently Lois. It represents tradition, an enclosed world, her setting, in a sense her antagonist, her sacrificial altar. It is one of the many Big Houses, as we call them in Ireland, that have traditionally represented to the "mere Irish" an alien garrison. English soldiers, men of the so-called, and self-called, army of occupation, will come here to play tennis. Lois has already danced on the avenue with a young subaltern, Gerald Lesworth. He will be shot by the Sinn Feiners. The house will go up in flames on the last page of its last September. Houses, outside and inside, are almost an obsession—for which we are truly grateful—with this writer. She does not often see them comfortably; she describes them effectively, even if more often than not she makes them *unheimlich*, overpowering. Here are two examples of the effect of impassive power that she extracts from her domestic interiors: Lois goes upstairs to join her cousin, Laurence, a young Oxford intellectual, her male counterpart, typical of many of Miss Bowen's men in that he is clever but ineffectual. He is reading in the ante-room because, characteristically, he is too lazy to climb a floor higher to his own room; he has, also characteristically, brought the wrong book with him; and he sits, characteristically, in "one of a circle of not very comfortable shellback chairs that no one took seriously". Lois, also characteristically, is often there chatting with him, her knee on a chair because "it is not worth while to sit down". (Symbolists may make what they like of these marks of ineffectuality in an *ante-room* through which other people are constantly passing about their business.) We read:

> "The high windows were curtainless; tasselled fringes frayed the light at the top. The white sills, the shutters folded back in their frames were blistered, as though the house had spent a day in the tropics. Exhausted by the sunshine, the backs of the crimson chairs were a thin light orange; a smell of camphor and animals drawn from skins on the floor by the glare of the morning still hung like dust on the evening chill. Going through to her room at nights Lois often tripped with her toe in the jaws of the tiger; a false step at any time sent some great claw skidding across the polish. Pale regimental groups, reunions a generation ago of the family or the neighbourhood gave out from the walls a vague depression. There were two locked bookcases of which the keys had been lost, and a troop of ebony elephants brought back from India by some one she did not remember paraded along the tops of the bookcases."

We become aware of dissolution, dissociation, a smother of dusty days no longer remembered, things faded and exhausted and threatened by the jaw of the moth. The traveller is forgotten, the keys are lost, the books unread, only the sun has force, and that to wither. It is in this ambience that the two young people converse, their lives before them in an exhausted house. A still more striking and explicit example occurs a little later when the guests and hosts are at dinner. "The distant ceiling imposed on consciousness its blank white oblong and a pellucid silence distilled from a hundred and fifty years of conversation waited beneath the ceiling." Can we feel anything but that the volition of these people is dwarfed by the emanations of the house? And may we not be fairly reminded of some Flaubertian interiors? A sapless place, we must certainly think, for any young girl. One could gather many such examples.

A third source of this sense of inertia is the grammar of the style: the use of the passive voice, the impersonal pronoun, the impersonal verb. "With him she felt committed by speech itself to a display of such unfathomable silliness that she might just as well come out with assertions surprising to herself." Felt committed, and so talks like an automaton. She had "a sense of return, of having been awaited". By what? By whom? Lady Naylor breaks off a pleasant chat because ... "There was life to go on with, the duty of love and pleasure fully discharged." Life is not actively enjoyed, it is to be "got on with"; and love and pleasure are something besides life. It is as if invisible angels in helicopters are directing the emotional traffic when Mrs Montmorency's mind "lay back in silence, but there was a kind of sentinel in her waiting for Hugo". Note how her past life with Hugo is described—as she sees it:

"Their life through which they went forward *uncertainly* without the *compulsion* of tragedy was *a net* of small complications. There was the *drag* of his *indecisions*, the fine snapping now and again of her minor *relinquishments*. Her health, his temperament, their varying poverty—they *were delayed, deflected*. She was *ordered* abroad for successive winters, to places he could not expect to endure."

It hits off a flaccid type, as it is intended to.

This use of grammar is pervasive for all the characters. "She gave so little answer to one's enquiry that one did not know how to approach." The impersonal pronoun is more than neutral. It is as chilling as an astral emanation. Lois excusing

herself says, as if she were talking about somebody else: "Panic
is beyond one." Here is passive, impersonal, and that house
which has more life than any of them, all together in two
sentences: "Lois *was sent* upstairs for the shawls; *it appeared*
that a touch of dew on the bare skin might be fatal. . . . On the
bare stairs *her feet found their* evening echoes; she dawdled,
listening." Again, in a lovely run of moods and images, when
they are all seated outside on the steps:

"Turning half around, she watched light breathe through the tips
of the cigarettes; it seemed as though everybody were waiting.
Night now held the trees with a toneless finality. The sky shone,
whiter than glass, fainting down to the fretted leaf-line, but was being
steadily drained by the dark below, to which the grey of the lawns,
like smoke, as steadily mounted. The house was highest of all with
toppling immanence like a cliff."

It is a most effective scene: the beleaguered party chatting lightly,
at rest, in the summer evening, under the tall façade of the house
until, suddenly, they hear the sound of a patrolling lorry,
furtive, sinister, "like some one running and crouching behind
a hedge". They retire, closing the doors for the night on the
impersonal danger.

This fabulous atmosphere as of people under a spell, as
marmoreal as a halted procession, fits the theme of this novel
perfectly. This was their very last autumnal stay in that house.
Fatality was in the offing. But fatality is always in the offing.
In *To the North* Markie Linkwater–another favoured type of
Miss Bowen's, the near cad–is literally thrown into Cecilia
Summers's lap: a jolting train brings them together in a dining
car. She had wished to be alone. As for him, he "never asked
more of women than affability; intimacy was shocking to him".
She is "mistrustful, tentative, uncertain". Identically, her friend
Emmeline had never wanted to become intimate with Julian
Summers. Myopic, over-serious, she has so far spent her years

"watching slip past her a blurred repetitive pattern she took to be life". Once, indeed, she had been kissed by a sailor on a battleship while looking up at Orion through a pair of opera-glasses, which he knocked out of her hand when he grabbed her. "Since the sailor she seemed to have been surrounded by shadowy people, acting without impulse, with no spring of passion in their behaviour, not throwing cracked opera-glasses as he did into the sea." As for Julian, he is without vitality, prefers inexact desires, is speculative and recessive. Once when another of Miss Bowen's favoured types, the demon-child, the *backfisch* at the lacy-drawers stage, is foisted on him for a week he suffers agonies of self-consciousness in her company. He sees that the poor child's approximation to what she thinks is naturalness is a parody of his own artificiality. She makes him feel as if somebody had scrubbed him clean, and all society becomes "a Turkish bath peopled by nudes". From her Julian flies to Cecilia for comfort: to be with her was to be in "dazzling ignorance of oneself" shrouded in an illusion of affection.

One may well imagine that such unenterprising types are less likely to step into the line of fate than to be drawn by its magnet. Their only hope of safety is to remain indoors. Even Saint John's Wood is a grave risk for such stay-at-home Red Riding Hoods. Wolves must be provided. That is the function of the near-cad. When he attaches himself to Emmeline he blinds her: she gives herself to him utterly. Unprepared for hazards, how could she be expected to know the ropes? Her passion frightens him. He wants to pull out. Doomed and joyless victim, she kills herself and him in a wild motor-drive at night to the Pole Star – *To the North*.

It is not, then, just one woman or two who move in the light of the fable. They are all touched by the spell. They all disguise under a mask of determination their interior surrender to the pressures of fate. One of her least assured novels is *Friends and*

Relations; it is one of her most revealing for the critic. Here Janet Studdert is introduced to us on the fourth page as "a heavy-lidded and rather sombre Diana", supervising the Wolf Cubs at her sister's wedding. Her sister marries one Edward Tilney, the son of Lady Elfrida Tilney, who had been divorced for adultery with a big-game hunter named Considine Meggatt of Batts Monachorum, a landed gentleman. Janet remains heavy-lidded and sombre throughout the book, but not at all Dianesque; indeed, as we gradually realise that she is the "heroine" we begin to observe that, far from being a huntress, she is being firmly propelled, half-awake, half-aware, like a beautiful white cow to some sacrificial altar somehow or other connected with her sister's marriage and with the big-game hunter. We see this when she becomes engaged, only six weeks after her sister's wedding, to the nephew of the wicked big-game hunter, Rodney Meggatt; for after many pages, many hints and ten years, it transpires that she had all along cherished a tender feeling for her sister's husband, Edward Tilney, and that he had cherished a tender feeling for her. She has—which is, to say the very least, highly extravagant and fanciful on her part—married the big-game hunter's nephew Rodney because this brings her vaguely into Edward Tilney's life on the slim ground that it was the wicked big-game hunter's affair with Lady Elfrida that broke Edward's childhood in two. This elaborate device to indicate the mesmeric nature of the force which governs Janet's will reveals to us the lengths to which Miss Bowen will go to deprive her characters of their autonomy.

"Early," she writes of the mesmerised Janet, "while her hair was still down her back she had accepted maturity; as though someone touching on her shoulder had told her to come away before the party had begun." To grow up is to submit to forces felt as inimical. Perhaps a week later, still unmarried, we are told: "These last weeks she had noticed someone who was herself for the first time, she could see nothing nowadays but herself, *a figure she watched with fatalism.*" Ten years later an unpleasant young woman who had observed the course of all those concerned in those two marriages wonders whether, somewhere, sometime Janet made a decision between a glance at and a glance away from Edward, and that from that moment "they both lived on *involuntarily*". Even when at long last she emerges from her trance-like state and faces the present and the past, we are told that "with impassive docility she lent herself to the retrospect". She faces the future in a similar mood, and she makes Edward see it in that mood, and as she speaks "she bends her head and looks into the palm of her hand like a Sybil".

It begins to appear that what is happening in all these stories is a clash between two aspects of life more easy to feel than to define. This bifrontine novelist sees life as two opposing forces. Shall we think of the clash as between innocence and knowledge? Youth and maturity? The dream and the actuality? Romance and that ordinary which we tend to call reality? The wish to be heroic and the nature of things which defeats heroism? Or the wish for peace and the desire for the battle? Certainly these unmotivated people seem to be drawn out of their safe harbourages by hypnotising fingers that they cannot resist. But just as the hypnotist cannot persuade his subject to act contrary to his subject's basic nature and basic will, we must believe that these people do not resist the hypnotising fingers only because they do not want to resist hard enough. They have at least some impulse to revolt. Somewhere beyond the enclosing piers, the familiar lighthouse, beyond the moaning bar they feel that there is something more worth while than where and as they are. They are timid but the pull is irresistible because, after all, it is within themselves, a power more elemental, more primordial than anything they have been taught or think they think. Night after night one or two of the marooned hear from far out beyond the lighthouse the old atavistic sirens call above the whisper of the ooze and the drip of the town's sewer-water. The pub-lights of the harbour are appealing, the galley is warm, people are playing bridge in the lighted villas on the hill, the Palais de Dance is neon-red, the radio is Light Programme. Yet, sooner or later a dark figure fumbles at a rope and puts out a boat. She will never return.

These novels are exquisitely composed logs of disaster, full of tender understanding, pity, and admiration for courage. They are also ruthless in their truth. With a sad *mouchoir* Miss Bowen waves her heroines over the cataract she has prepared for them. This is sad – because these young people are not Emma Bovarys asking for impossible experiences. They ask only for the simplest things – honest feeling, sympathy, trust, love. Is one to understand that these things are unattainable in modern society? If so, what, one asks, has gone wrong? It is pretty much the question that all these writers of the Twenties[1] ask and answer, each in his own way. One could consider Miss Bowen as a tragic obverse of Evelyn Waugh.

Nowhere is the clash more explicitly and movingly stated than in *The Death of the Heart*, surely her best novel. The period is the late Thirties. Thomas and Anna Quayne are a childless couple, aged about thirty-six and thirty-four. They are prosperous; they have three servants, live in an urban stucco-house facing Regent's Park, could be envied, should be happy. One cannot, however, escape the effect of the words chosen in the

[1] *The Last September* is placed in the years 1920 and 1921. *Friends and Relations*: part One is dated "192–"; part Two is ten years later. *To the North* is not dated but is clearly post-1918. In *The Death of the Heart* Thomas Quayne and his wife Anna were born in 1900 and 1902, or within a year one side or the other of those dates. Stella of *The Heat of the Day* is "a year or two younger than the century". They are all people who came to their majority in the Twenties.

opening pages to describe the sort of desirable Regency house
in which they live:

"At the far side of the road dusk set the Regency buildings back
at a *false* distance: against the sky they were *colourless silhouettes,
insipidly* ornate, *brittle and cold*. The blackness of windows not yet
lit or curtained made the houses look *hollow inside*."

Thomas's father, an idealistic, sentimental old buffer, would
have been just up Mr Waugh's street–the typical, futile,
fumbling bourgeois who would sign Peace Pledges every week
and would in a couple of years be acclaiming Mr Chamberlain,
and probably behave like a brave man under the bombs. At
the age of fifty-seven he had committed adultery with a fluffy
young widow named Irene and, much to his dismay, been
cheerfully packed off to the Continent with her by his wife.
Irene bore a child, Portia, now an orphan, aged sixteen. She
has been sent to stay with Thomas and Anna by her dying father.
"He had felt," Anna explains dryly to a friend, "that Portia
had grown up exiled not only from her own country but from
normal, cheerful family life." She adds, uncomfortably, that
"he idealised us rather, you see". (Symbolists may decide why
the child was called Portia. She does seem to sit in judgement on
Thomas and Anna, in her lonely and agonising longing for
"normal, cheerful family life", her "impossible lovingness and
austere trust"). And yet these two must have seemed wholly
normal to everybody else. We have met them thousands of
times, an upright, well-meaning, refined couple, eager to be
kind and civilised towards everyone. The child's hunger for
affection is too much for them; too much for that brittle, cold,
colourless, hollow house that they think of as a home, "shuttered
and muffled" against the noise of the city, where the lamplight
binds the room "in unreal circles", where the heart shines only
with the sterile glow of an electric fire. (I am, of course, trans-
lating, and therefore destroying, the subtle suggestiveness of an

artist who uses her words with the most delicate implications. She does not say any of these things. They pass imperceptibly into us as part of the poignant mood she elicits, touch after touch, from our sensibilities. The only grave criticism one might make is that she does make her characters feel at a higher level than their own sensibilities.)

In the end Portia feels betrayed by everybody except the dour old family servant Matchett, who though dour is still "natural". She is betrayed especially by Eddie, the near-cad, whom she is drawn to love, or to imagine she loves, but who pities her rather than loves her, seeing in her another victim of the world he also, but more frankly, fears and hates and tries to be spry enough to cope with. There can be no question as to what these two young people symbolise. They, though primarily Portia, represent an excess of innocence that, with a foolhardiness possible only in the pure of heart, constantly affronts what Miss Bowen significantly calls "the system of our affections", which is "too corrupt" for innocence and therefore shatters it. In this world where life is (her word) always "edited" by this corrupt system anything which is unedited is doomed. "Why," Eddie says passionately to Portia—and it is a cry which all the writers of the Twenties, and since, assume to be justified—"why should we be at the start of our two lives when everything around us is losing its virtue? How can we grow up when there's nothing left to inherit, when what we have to feed on is stale and corrupt?" And when Thomas is made to think that "society was self-interest given a pretty gloss", a web of calculation where only love, he hoped, was uncalculated, we have to see that by love he does not mean charity but merely an emotion likewise centred on himself, or at most on one other person. There is no place in such a world for Portia, for anybody so "thorough", so absolute, so honest.

Even Eddie, her fellow odd-man-out, cannot put up with

her absoluteness. In exasperation he says to her towards the end: "You expect every bloody thing to be right or wrong, and to be done with the whole of oneself." And: "All the other women I've known but you, Portia, seem to know what to expect, and that gives me something to go on. I don't care how wrong they are: it gets one along." Again: "Because I said I loved you you expect me to be as sweet to you as my mother. You're damned lucky to have somebody even as innocent as I am. . . ." Inevitably we begin to see the joke of it all. Portia is so tragic that she becomes comic. Young acquaintances tell her she is bats. A twist of the globe and, like her papa, she would be a figure for Evelyn Waugh. But by another twist she and Eddie would be fit for Graham Greene, another Rose, another Pinkie. And indeed such innocence as hers has to be thought "bats" by this workaday world of ours or we are all either bats or criminals, as we possibly are whenever we are being worldly. The force of this book is that it says, firmly: "Choose!" It puts things up to us. It is at the same time an enormous tribute to Miss Bowen's sense of proportion, as well as to her technical skill in wisely lowering the temperature for a while, that she can, for a whole central stretch of the novel, overlay the subject with a humour that never diminishes our sympathy with Portia, never allows us to forget that hearts break every day with a grin.

Let us call the clash a clash between the world and the blind values of unspoiled youth. These novels are written in sorrowing admiration, perhaps even in envy of youth, that age of dreams when alone truth is whole and faith is utter and hopes are unbroken and love is perfect, that age which is so "impossible" to us elders, when love is impossibly romantic, too dramatic, misled, misplaced, hopelessly exaggerated–and which leads to fatality whenever adults try to live out their youthful honesty in this inimical social world. Miss Bowen is all on the side of what youth believes, but she is a worldly woman, and she

knows that it does not work, and her characters have to pay
for her pleasure in wishing that it might work. Like Flaubert
she is relentless in the end. She differs from him only as an
Irishwoman's sentiment differs from a Frenchman's intelligence,
so that she sighs more audibly as she snaps the frail threads of
hopeless innocence.

In *The House in Paris* the following revealing passage suggests
an *idée maîtresse*:

"... young girls like the excess of any quality. Without knowing
it they want to suffer, to suffer they must exaggerate; they like to
have loud chords struck on them. Loving art better than life they
need men to be actors; only an actor moves them, with his telling
smile, undomestic, out of touch with the everyday that they dread.
They love to enjoy love as a system of doubts and shocks. They are
right: not seeking husbands yet they have no reason to see love
socially. This natural fleshly protest against good taste is broken down
soon enough; their natural love of the cad is outwitted by their
mothers. Vulgarity, inborn like original sin, unfolds with the woman
nature, unfolds ahead of it quickly and has a flamboyant flowering
in the young girl. ..."

There are many of these young girls, in Miss Bowen's novels,
these flamboyant roses, overgrown, "vulgar", undomestic,
not giving a damn about worldly good taste, over-romantic,
passionate in a leggy way, rebelliously indifferent to love as
Mamma sees it, suffering, and adept at making others suffer too;
young monsters, as they seem to us weary, middle-aged, self-
cosseting elders who have long since forgotten the miseries
of our youth. It is only when we see them lacerating themselves
that we remember, and thank God that the beastly business of
being young is over. They are Theodora and Dorothea in
Friends and Relations, Pauline in *To the North*, Henrietta in
The House in Paris. (Leopold, in the same novel, is a male
counterpart, and he is more of a girl than a boy–but I do not

think Miss Bowen knows about boys as she does about girls.)
They appear in many of the short stories. The girl in "The Parrot"
will grow up to be one of these vulgarians. She will grow up to
suffer. For it is these girls who grow up to be Miss Bowen's
doomed heroines. They still enjoy love for its shocks and
doubts. They have a weakness for the cad. They exaggerate,
do not seek husbands, refuse to think socially. The large question,
indeed, about the Bowenesque heroine is whether she is ever
truly adult. Carnally and sentimentally her women are in-
continently involved in the toils of their own adolescence. They
go on dreaming too long. So Karen, in *The House in Paris*,
thinks when she had crossed her line of fate that this was something that should have happened long ago, and seems to think
too that now she can, having poured the libation, return to her
normal life. She says to her lover: "You and I are the dream."
He promptly kills himself.

Elizabeth Bowen is a romantic up against the despotism of
reality. So many other Irish writers are. The metallic brilliance,
even the occasional jarring brassiness and jauntiness of her style
is, in an admirable sense, a fake, a deceptive cocoon wrapped
about the central precious, tender thing. One could imagine
a hare settling into her form, a sticky little leveret between her
paws, or perhaps a lioness growling over her young. It is the
growl of *Ich grolle nicht*, the Flaubertian coldness imposed on
Irish feeling, and the theme is so heart-breaking that it would
be embarrassing if she were not tight-lipped about those
heroines who just do not know what o'clock it is once love
enters their unwary lives. She writes of romantic heroines in an
age that has made the two words pejorative. The underlying
assumptions here are very much of the Twenties. The conflicts
are no longer clear enough to justify bold affirmations, positive
statements of loyalty, straight fights or declared aims or ends.
Miss Bowen's heroines are, after all, always defeated. In

Mauriac's phrase their beauty is borrowed from despair. Not, as we have seen, that she is anti-heroic, but that she must state coldly that heroism, the absolute aim, does not stand a chance in modern society, even while she still insists passionately that it is always worth while to try. She has not assumed that we must therefore reject tradition, but she is plainly unenthusiastic about it. She does not assume that violence is the only possible alternative in fiction to thought. She does not assume that the intellect must be abdicated by the modern novelist. She hovers patiently over her subjects. But the prime technical characteristic of her work, as of other modern women writers, such as Virginia Woolf, is that she fills the vacuum which the general dis-integration of belief has created in life by the pursuit of sensibility. It is a highly sophisticated pursuit. Sometimes it is over-conscious and overdone.

Her sensibility can be witty; it can also be catty, even brassy, too smart like an over-clever *décor* for a ballet. I do not mind that it is, to my taste, on occasion vulgar, though not quite in the sense in which her young girls are vulgar. She has defended, or at least pleaded, for sympathy with vulgarity, and are there not times when good taste is itself a little vulgar? One thinks of the ghastly good taste of Mr Charles Morgan. But what one means by finding this kind of good taste rather vulgar is that it is bloodless, and that one longs occasionally for a good, warm, passionate howl like an Italian mother baying over her dead child. This sort of earthiness is outside the range of any English-trained writer. When Elizabeth Bowen is dealing with elemental things she skirts around them with too much elegance. There are certain things she will not deign to describe. The actual falling in love of her people is one. So that if one feels that tragedy is a race where one has to take one's fences must one not feel that there is a bit too much *dressage* about *The Heat of the Day*?

The one place where she is really earthy is when she is being humorous, and would, many times over, that she were humorous more often, for when she is being humorous she is also most human. Louie in *The Heat of the Day* is not only good fun but real; down to earth; far more so than Robert, Harrison and Stella pirouetting about each other exhaustingly. Yet, to take a fair measure of the humanity (as against the elegance) of her sensibilities, one may compare them with the sensibilities of Virginia Woolf whose antennae are as sensitive as remote radar, but who reacts not so much to human beings as to things and "states of mind". Miss Bowen is also responsive to things and states of mind, but she responds chiefly, and warmly, to her own favoured types of people. "Things," Mrs Woolf characteristically makes Terence Hewitt say in *The Voyage Out*, "things I feel come to me like lights. I want to combine them. Have you ever seen fireworks that make figures? I want to make figures." That also, to my taste, is a form of vulgarity through elegance. Miss Bowen would never be quite so refined. She wants to make people not figures, to put them into conflict with society, and her explorations of their feelings are never just an exploitation of her own.

Her outer-imposed limitations do, nevertheless, obtrude themselves. *The Death of the Heart* was, indeed, a firm and passionately felt protest against the modern desiccation of feeling, but one could not help noting that it offered no moral approach to the problem: meaning that it intimated no norm to set against the subnormal. But can one reasonably blame Miss Bowen for this? We are brought back by this longing for a norm to the death of the traditional Hero, that symbol of the norm in all traditional literature. She, too, can only present us with the martyr in place of the Hero, the representative not of the norm but of the disease. Greene's alternative is God. Miss Bowen is too deeply rooted in the great, central humanist

tradition of European culture to take refuge in hereafters. What
she directs our eyes towards is the malady of our times that
breaks the dreaming and gallant few. It is what her master
Flaubert did with Emma Bovary, more ruthlessly. She has
described the dilemma of our times honestly, beautifully and
at times movingly. To have done so much, and done it so
well, is to have done a great deal.

VIRGINIA WOOLF
and JAMES JOYCE

or

Narcissa and Lucifer

I

Since Joyce was born in 1882, published *Chamber Music* in 1907, *Dubliners* in 1914, *A Portrait of the Artist as a Young Man* in 1916, and *Ulysses* in 1922, he has no place chronologically among a group of writers who came to their majority in the Twenties.[1] *Ulysses* must, however, have had a large influence on the period, and I suspect that even Virginia Woolf, who disliked it, was not unaffected by its technique when writing *The Waves* and *Between the Acts*. But I am putting the two together for other reasons. I think it may be profitable to contrast Mrs Woolf's "moments of vision" with Joyce's "epiphanies"; to compare his metaphysical view of reality with her rather simpler viewpoint; and to place both in the tradition of individualistic revolt against the order of nature and society which is so evident in all fiction in our time. I am also collocating these two writers in order to force a question which I have held back until this last essay, and which, putting it very simply, is to ask whether any literature can be in health and vigour without some form of faith.

To explain what I mean by faith I will begin by quoting from Mr Richard Blackmur's essay on "The Later Poetry of Yeats" from his volume *The Expense of Greatness*:[2]

[1] I am indebted in this essay to Hugh Kenner's "*The Portrait* in Perspective," from *James Joyce: Two Decades of Criticism* (New York, 1948).
[2] *The Expense of Greatness*. New York, 1940, p. 75.

"Poetry does not flow from thin air but requires always a literal faith, an imaginative faith, or, as in Shakespeare, a mind full of provisional faiths. The life we all live is not alone enough of a subject for a serious artist; it must be life with a leaning, life with a tendency to shape itself only in certain forms, to afford its most lucid revelations only in certain lights. If our final interest, both as poets or as readers, is in the reality declared when the forms have been removed and the lights taken away, yet we never come to the reality at all without the first advantage of the forms and the lights. Without them we should see nothing, but only glimpse something unstable. . . . So it was with the early Yeats; his early poems are fleeting, some of them beautiful and some that sicken, as you read them, to their own extinction. But as he acquired for himself a discipline, however unacceptable to the bulk of his readers, his poetry obtained an access of reality. . . . It is almost the mark of the poet of genuine merit in our time . . . that he performs his work in the light of an insight, a group of ideas, and a faith, with the discipline that flows from them, which, taken together, form a view of life which most readers cannot share, and which, furthermore, most readers feel as repugnant, or sterile, or simply inconsequential. All this is to say . . . that our culture is incomplete with regard to poetry. . . ."

Clearly, Mr Blackmur does not mean, as I certainly do not mean, by Faith any schematised set of dogmatic beliefs held, or expected to be held, by a mass of people in common. Indeed, the essay points out that Yeats could write in a state of exaltation unrelated to any concord or system ("All Souls Night"), as he could exploit bare emotion without reference to character ("A Deep Sworn Vow"); and it further stresses that poetry may rely on evanescent conventions. The example Mr Blackmur gives is not *Othello*, but it could well have been in so far as jealousy in our time is not, apart from certain unregenerate Latin countries, as powerfully savage and elemental an emotion as it once was. The burthen of the essay is the constructional use that Yeats made of the political and mythological hieroglyphs or forms offered to him by Ireland; and it concerns itself, over all, with the superstructure he built for his emotions out of magical lore. A faith, then, for literary purposes, means any feeling for life or any way of seeing life which is coherent, persistent, inclusive and forceful enough to give organic form to the totality of a writer's work.

To apply this, I doubt if anybody who has studied the totality of Virginia Woolf's work can have failed to sense that, for all its manifold flashes of acute feeling, her abiding weakness was her inability–of which she herself was not unaware–so to feel life, so to write about it that form would grow into her work as a child's bones grow into the original frail embryo conceived in passion.

When, in art, the word is made flesh it is also made bone. "The idea," Flaubert thought, "is born of the form." It would seem to me more reasonable to say that form is born of the idea, or that the idea can only express itself in form, but the two, Flaubert rightly felt, are inseparable. It is as if the concept which strikes the artist takes flesh in his mind in terms of shapes which, in turn, impress themselves on his page or his canvas, and are then the apparently inevitable organic expression of his first emotion. They are coincident or congruent with it. This apparently inevitable organic form is, I must insist on thinking, quite different from the stuck-on form of *Ulysses*, where the classical reference is either a technical preconception or a post-rationalisation, except in so far as Bloom and Stephen may, possibly, have been felt from the beginning as a classical Father-in-search-of-Son theme. And, even so, is the form not apparent as something forced on rather than emergent from the material itself? On the other hand the form of Faulkner's *Light in August* is organic form. It was inherent. It has all the appearances of inevitability. One does not feel that the dual myth, of Cain and Babel, was chosen, preconceived, rationally imposed. It has all the appearances of having arisen in Faulkner's imagination simultaneously with whatever passing experience in actual life excited him to start writing. In that flash he conceived a theme and it, literally, took shape. By contrast when I say that *For Whom the Bell Tolls* leaves no clear arc behind it in the sky of the mind I mean that Hemingway had not fully realised what he wanted his experience to mean.

Form and meaning, then, or form and faith (in the sense in which I have understood faith) are very close to one another. Form is a descent of the Holy Ghost on the soul ready to receive it. It is an epiphany, a manifestation, a showing-forth, a tongue of fire, after which the apostle can speak "in divers tongues the wonderful works of God". In literature the descent can come from pure genius, a lightning-flash of intuition when we see into the souls of things; or it can come, more painfully, through a combination of intelligence and sensibility when an artist winds his way into the heart of his subject. In the one event, as with Wordsworth, the result may be the gradual development of a growing, and possibly integrated, body of faith—again in our sense of that word. Examples of the second process range from Ben Jonson to Conrad, from Donne to Eliot: a faith—again in the literary sense—brought to bear on the subject so deliberately, so wilfully that it is often the writer's business to give the opposite impression, to conceal, that is, his *a priori* slant or attitude.

Now, if Mrs Woolf so rarely achieved organic form I suggest that the reason is that she was unable to deduce "an insight, a group of ideas" from her experience of life. She remained to the end so intoxicated by the wonder-making variety of the universe that she never achieved a position of intellectual or emotional equipoise in relation to outer reality, and so never won control over herself or over her material. She never constructed her Faith. She never achieved Form. Moore said that Pater's meaning was often lost in the folds of his style.

Mrs Woolf's ultimate meaning is constantly lost in the folds of her sensibility, and of her Narcissism.

But we must not use terms like "reality", "control", "constructed", or "sensibilities" without some effort at definition.

I write these pages in a room which has a bay-window of four sections. If I rise from my desk and look out through the left-hand section, I may record in my mind that—"I see the quadrangle." I do not, in fact, see the quadrangle. I see only a portion of it. What I see, furthermore, is a portion of the quad isolated within the frame of this section of my window. This frame encloses a form of picture—the tower, a tree, some grass, some stone, some windows, a student who has paused and is reading a letter, a segment of the sky and some clouds. Since all these things are artificially related to one another by being framed, I see not only those various things but am aware of their pictorial relationship which changes them from facts to forms, eloquent now through their relationship. Moreover, I am aware of certain memories and associations that they evoke. Thus, when the hot-water pipes clink, these related shapes, inexplicably, cause me to imagine that I hear a black-smith's anvil in an Irish village many miles away. (Proust went fully into this aspect of vision.) Much else that I remember, though I do not explicitly define my memories, is part of my experience as I look out of my window "at the quadrangle". For my outward glance has by this time become an emotional experience. Patently, if I wished to record the essence of this slight experience I could not put it all in, as, often, Mrs Woolf so passionately wished she could. I must select, as she fully realised and said. The crucial question arises: By what canon do I select?

Consider, for example, alone, how far Time is involved, Time which involves knowledge, not merely springing from my own personal memories but from racial and atavistic

memories that are every man's inheritance, and which willy-nilly
become part of that minute experience of looking from my
study window. Vision, it seems then, is not alone a sensory or
emotional experience; it is also an intellectual decision, or
choice, or selection in response to the invitation or challenge of
what we see. No experience can be otherwise since it is, in
effect, part of that perpetual process of wedding the Subject (I)
with the Object (the Not I), unless, by some fierce negation,
akin to barbarism, a man blots out whole portions of his
intellectual being. (Faulkner seems to have managed to do this.)
This wedding, this interfusion, this suture, a co-penetrative
process like to the sexual act, sometimes spoken of as the
"knowing" a woman, alerts within us a communication with
the significance embedded in outer reality which is, in the
ultimate, a participation in some essence common to both the
person who experiences and the mode of his experience. It is for
this essence that we are always seeking, selectively; the element
common to the thing and to us; that which, as we say, makes
the thing meaningful to us. We exist in ourselves, that is, only
when we have existed in others. We do not hold the mirror up
to nature. Nature holds the mirror up to us.

> For speculation turns not to itself
> Until it hath travelled and is mirrored there
> Where it may see itself. . . .

I am insisting, it will be seen, that every artist's communication
with life is not only an emotional and intellectual act but a
moral act. It is what Simone Weil said of all created beauty: it
is an entry into the mouth of the labyrinth at whose centre (in
her symbolism) God is waiting to eat us up; or, in more secular
language, at whose core we are merged with the mystery, or
meaning, of all life, all reality, and in some degree partake of
it—unless, to be sure, we are writing best-sellers.

Now, in her own way, Mrs Woolf acknowledged and asserted

all this. The end of the journey, she saw, is certainly not just photographic or naturalistic reproduction. Realism, as the word goes, for its own pure or impure sake was, to her, just "waste". But how far did she realise that when outer reality is inwardly recreated it becomes hypostasised? Into what it is changed nobody can say, but changed it is. Proust would say that it is distilled into essences, and a Thomist could probably find common ground with him, saying that the end of all art is reached when the artist has so played about with the accidents of experience as to reveal its essence. But these are no more than wordy efforts to express our awareness of the change. My feeling is that Mrs Woolf fell into the very impasse she detested: that she did not change her experience at all, but that she did record and reproduce most delicately, yet quite natural-istically the externals of life. It is indeed true that the fleshly envelope of life which she wished to dissolve, to make luminous, becomes often much less opaque than it had been—this we gratefully acknowledge—yet it remains as she found it. That "access of reality" which came to the later Yeats as he achieved a form of discipline, "in the light of an insight, a group of ideas, a faith . . . a view of life" continued to evade her. And this is why, finally, I have spoken of her sensibilities and her Narcissism; because I think that she was too absorbed in her private self to wed experience fully. She could not give herself utterly. It always happens when our sensibilities are too hotly pursued. The Subject (or ego) is over-emphasised; the Object is under-emphasised; the enemy lying in wait is subjectivity.

It is fascinating, and sometimes depressing, to watch her groping with this only half-understood problem. When writing *The Waves*, which she originally intended to call *The Moths*, she wrote in her Diary:

"I mean to eliminate all waste, deadness, superfluity, to give the moment whole; whatever it includes. Say that the moment is a combination of thought, sensation, the voice of the sea. Waste, deadness, come from the inclusion of things that don't belong to the moment; this appalling narrative business of the realist; getting on from lunch to dinner; it is false, unreal, merely conventional. Why admit anything to literature that is not poetry, by which I mean saturated? Is that not my grudge against the novelists? That they select nothing? The poets succeeded by simplifying; practically everything is left out. I want to put practically everything in: yet to saturate. That is what I want to do in *The Moths*. It must include nonsense, fact, sordidity, but made transparent."

Four pages after deciding "to put practically everything in" she decided: "I shall do away with exact place and time. Anything may be out of the window–a ship–a desert–London." She had only momentary realisations of the fact that her real enemy was herself, that she was caught in the individualist's impasse of what, in the following passage, she calls "the damned egotistical self". One could ponder long on the misconceptions of this entry in her Diary. I italicise the phrases which arrest me:

"This afternoon arrived at some idea of a new form for a new novel. Suppose one thing should open out of another–as in an unwritten novel–only not for ten pages but for two hundred or so–doesn't that give the looseness and lightness I want? Doesn't that get closer and yet keep *form* and speed, and enclose everything, everything? *What the unity shall be I have yet to discover; the theme is a blank to me* . . . I suppose the danger is the damned egotistical self *which ruins Joyce and Richardson to my mind.* . . ."

This egotistical self seems very much to the fore in another entry:

"I am now and then haunted by some semi-mystic, very profound life of a woman which should all be told on one occasion; and time shall be utterly obliterated; future shall somehow blossom out of the past. One incident–say the fall of a flower–might contain it. My theory being that *the actual event practically does not exist*, nor time either."

There is one crucial passage in the Diary. It is, in the literal sense, one of those agnostic confessions which gives us a troubling insight into the heart of her dilemma:

"Why is there not a discovery in life? Something one could lay hands on and say, 'This is it.' My depression is a harassed feeling. I'm looking–but that's not it, that's not it. What is it? And I shall die before I find it? Then (as I was walking in Russell Square last night) I see the mountains in the sky; the great clouds; and the moon which is risen over Persia. I have a great and astonishing sense of something there which is 'it'. It's not exactly beauty that I mean. It is that the thing is in itself enough, satisfactorily achieved. A sense of my own strangeness, walking on the earth is there too; of the infinite oddity of the human position; trotting along Russell Square with the moon up there and those mountain clouds. Who am I; what am I; and so on. . . ."

If it were not for the whole context of her life one might dismiss this as anybody's casual mock-serious, "What does it all mean?" Knowing her prevailing attitude to life, we see a sensitive, serious, delicate-minded woman, the daughter of Sir Leslie Stephen, the eminent Cambridge rationalist, who had been married to Thackeray's daughter, known almost every distinguished writer of his era–she was the god-daughter of James Russell Lowell, Meredith is said to have fallen in love with her when she was ten–walking in Russell Square (that is to say, looking out of *her* study window) and not so much not knowing what she sees as not seeing it at all. Clouds and the moon. Narcissa involved in her own strangeness all her life. Subject and Object far from at peace with one another. The experience is certainly not intellectual, though she may think of it as "mystical". (The event practically does not exist, nor Time either.) Russell Square does not exist. It does not radiate out in associations, or into any accepted traditions, is not firmly seated in what we must call the forms of society, has, in short, so little sense of fixture or solidity that the moon is over Ispahan.

Certainly this daughter of the great Victorians will not want to write novels about any sort of real, accepted world. (She was to try it, once, in *The Years*, a novel that almost broke her, and which is the least characteristic of all her books, and can only be counted a sad failure–for her.) She and where she was could never have been a unity. No wonder she can say: "When I write I am merely a sensibility." And add: "Sometimes I like being Virginia, but only," she goes on rather disapprovingly, "when I'm scattered, and various and gregarious."

Once she records a snatch of conversation with Lytton Strachey:

"Strachey: And the novel?
"Virginia: Oh, I put in my hand and rummage in the branpie.
"Strachey: Yes, that's what's so wonderful, and it's all different!
"Virginia: Yes, I'm twenty people. . . ."

What order, form, method, meaning, significance, one must wonder, can possibly be won by the branpie method?

Her Bloomsbury friends, one fears, were, like Strachey, too much too evasive, polite and kind. But one gave her a clear pointer to her difficulty, and with her usual honesty she saw the point. When Roger Fry told her that she was over-doing the prose-lyric vein, she saw the truth and force of the criticism. "I poetise my inanimate scenes, stress my personality, *don't let the meaning emerge from the matière*." It was the outward symptom of her inability to come to terms with actuality, to give it a fair "do", to cut down her ration of "personality". Here, for example, is an allegedly prose passage describing a woman (Mrs Dalloway) sewing by the window of her home in London (I print it for what it really is–*vers libre*):

Quiet descended on her, calm, content, as her needle
Drawing the silk smoothly to its gentle pause,
Collected the green folds together,
And attached them very lightly to the belt.

So, on a summer's day,
Waves collect, overbalance and fall;
Collect and fall;
And the whole world seems to be saying, that is all,
More and more ponderously,
Until even the heart in the body which lies in the sun
On the beach, says too, that is all.
Fear no more, says the heart.
Fear no more says the heart, committing its burthen to some sea
Which sighs collectively
For all sorrows,
And renews, begins, collects, lets fall.
And the body alone listens to the passing bee. . . .

"Have I the power of conveying the true reality? Or do I write essays about myself?" Her self-questioning is ruthless. And she did not always write essays about herself. There were many blessed moments, a great many, when she did humbly bed with common things and in forgetting herself in their arms revealed herself as well as them:

"The snow, which had been falling all night, lay at three o'clock in the afternoon over the field and the hill. Clumps of withered grass stood out upon the hill-top; the furze-bushes were black, and now and then a black shiver crossed the snow as the wind drove flurries of frozen particles before it. The sound was of a broom sweeping-sweeping."

That is nature holding the mirror up to the artist: a beautiful picture of Virginia Woolf. It is an enchanting pause set in the flow of life, like standing on a stepping-stone for a second to glance at the stream at one's feet, a brief, of necessity brief moment of personal ecstasy, a summary of, a purification of the perpetual flux of common things.

What did Virginia Woolf, in any broadest possible sense of the word, "believe" in terms of the most provisional "faith"? I think she believed chiefly, like all that Cambridge set who were her friends, in the revelatory possibilities of "states of mind".

Recall her first novel, *The Voyage Out*. Helen and Ridley Ambrose, Clarissa and Richard Dalloway, and Rachel Vinrace the Ambroses' niece are on a ship bound for a resort in South America. Throughout Mrs Woolf seems to speak through her characters. So, Rachel, a young idealist, much bewildered by the ways of the world, when kissed by Dalloway is assured that "the common fleshly reality of all this is insignificant". She will meet Terence Hewett in San Marina and form an attachment so high-minded that it will come to nothing. Thus, when they see another pair of lovers kissing, Terence says: "Their lives are now changed for ever." Rachel says: "I could almost burst into tears." Terence says: "There's something horribly pathetic about it, I agree." (This could be funny, but it is not meant to be.) Terence wants to write a novel about silence; that is, about the things people do not say. He says:

"What I want to do in writing novels is very much what you want to do when you play the piano. . . . We want to find out what's behind things, don't we? Look at the lights down there scattered about anyhow. Things, I feel, come to me like lights. I want to combine them. I want to make figures." (Which is very much what the author so often seems to be doing.)

He again seems to speak for her when he says: "There's no difficulty in conceiving incidents; the difficulty is to put them into shape—not to get run away with." Or, when uttering a preference for writing about the past, he says that it detaches one from modern conditions so that one can make one's characters "more abstract than people who live as we do". Rachel, I feel, is also reflecting her author when she says: "Does it ever seem to you, Terence, that the world is composed entirely of vast blocks of matter and that we're nothing but patches of light?"

How acute E. M. Forster was when he said that he liked this book not for its people but because it was "vague and universal". In fact, he did not like the characters; but then he "felt no need to care for them". The adjectives are just: the book is one long series of vague and universal "states of mind" in which common lives become so many "patches of light". In the end when Mrs Woolf gives her heroine an infection of which she dies we feel that our pleasure in common life–in the young girl's voyage out into the world, her early love, her youthful discoveries–is cruelly and wantonly smacked in the face. In the last sentence the despised order of common life is sent, almost contemptuously, on its routine way–the old people in the hotel "picking up their books, their cards, their balls of wool, their work-baskets, and passing [him] one after another on their way to bed".

With her background and upbringing, surrounded by a highly intellectual, cultured, kindly, civilised but, in the end, rather drearily rationalist set, it is hard to see what Mrs Woolf could have believed in except in some such concept of life as a chimera lit by moments of sensory joy. The sound of the snow like a broom sweeping, sweeping. . . . Steamers in a fog resounding like gigantic tuning-forks. . . . Cabbage-leaves in the moonlight. . . . Memories coming back and back like a sleeper jolting against one in a railway-carriage. . . .

She was at her best in *The Waves* and *Between the Acts*, for two totally opposite reasons. In her last novel she found one solution for her problem of subjective involvement–comedy. In *The Waves* she virtually abandoned all effort at objectivity or detachment. She let the subjective reins fall loosely on the neck of her Pegasus and wrote a frank elegy on innocence and idealism. If one wishes to enjoy *The Waves* one should go at once from the first section where the children are playing to the last section which explicitly gives the key to the many revealing, or would-be revealing, moments too lightly touched as they fall throughout the body of the story. "We had lost," said the extrovert and gregarious Bernard, "what they had kept." One may skip the stuck-on interludes about the waves: these are feeble efforts to simulate form.

At bottom, her trouble was one to which she was fully alive. "Who thinks it? And am I outside the thinker?"

It was a proper question for a novelist; it is not, we should point out to those who sometimes try to turn her into a prose-poet, a proper question for a poet. The Seer and the Seen is quite on another plane from the Thinker and the Thought. A poet may do what a novelist may not do, so lose himself in the natural world that the natural world seems to be speaking with its own voice, its own life, its own mind: as in, say, Blake's *The Book of Thel* when the daughter of the Seraphim speaks:

> *Art thou a Worm? Image of weakness, art thou but a Worm?*
> *I see thee like an infant wrapped in the Lilly's leaf. . . .*

Such a self-merging, so direct a self-identification, with so unmediated a presence as the result, is not possible in prose which, by reason of its function, one might say because of its mental temperature, is obliged to observe from the distance of thought or consideration. And so it becomes the urgent problem of the novelist to find out how he may experience fully and yet not surrender or evade thought, or, at least, not appear to do so, while enjoying or suffering that full experience. To revert to the sexual metaphor that I have already used more than once, if a man does not, or cannot, surrender cerebral consciousness in love he will experience not a perfect union but an incomplete union terribly close to auto-eroticism; and instead of writing afterwards about total love he will be able only to write of his own isolated thoughts and sensations. From this self or cerebral consciousness there is no release, no escape except through that abnormal duality of the novelist's mind which provides him with what Freud might call a latent censor who records in his unconscious being the nature of experiences of which at the time his consciousness makes no record at all. Long after he has left the battlefield, the gaming-table, the bed, the cataract, the sociable dinner-table, the river's brim, the quiet wood, the crowded street, there rise to his memory things he never re-membered, words he never heard, images he never saw. His memory is partly creative because it is partly selective, because his censor is his second-self, because this second-self, which never sleeps, is like seeking like, incessantly. Then, with thought-ful awareness, he will re-select, arrange, shape, and by shaping state; but not until then, at the risk of an excessive subjectivity, intellectualism, devitalisation, or the mere self-delineation of the Narcissist locked up in his own ego.

2

In Joyce's work who thinks it? And is the writer outside the thinker? Does he really sit on the clouds paring his nails in godlike indifference to the doings of his characters? I suggest that he is not in the least detached, that he is, on the contrary, closely involved, both emotionally and intellectually, in the doings of all his characters. We may test this most easily by considering his first two novels.

Let us grant, to begin with, that total detachment is impossible to any writer who lives, as he must, imaginatively into his material. (Stendhal, for example, is patently woven into all his major characters.) Grant, further, that such detachment as we think we observe, are persuaded to observe, is an illusion on two planes. There is the illusion of unobtrusiveness achieved by technical skill, the author's cloak of invisibility; and there is the illusion of impartiality achieved by intellectual discipline. Now, it is plain that with Joyce the first illusion is constantly at war with the second. Far from making an effort to persuade us that he is not present in his novels, he indicated frankly by the title of his first novel that he is his own subject. It is true that when we first saw this novel, on its original appearance, we partially accepted the title as a sort of double-bluff, or even as a simple trick to give an illusion of actuality; as when a novelist writes a story in the form of a first-person diary. We could, at that date, go a long way towards accepting the flimsy disguises, make a gesture of accepting the book as purely imaginative. But *Ulysses*, and everything we have since learned about Joyce and his techniques, put an end to that. The reader is now in the position that he cannot tell, without much study, where autobiography ends and fiction begins.

Joyce may have foreseen this danger. For it is a danger to persuasiveness. We do not question the imagination, we allow it great liberties, but we do question that which is not a product of the imagination. He might well have foreseen, then, that in putting himself into his novel he was laying a special strain on our sympathy. He might have foreseen that we might fear that we were being "got at" through a ventriloquist's dummy called Stephen Dedalus. And it is true that we will always be slow, or actually may cease to give our assent to any book where we feel that the characters are not autonomous, but are being manipulated by a marionette-master. (This, I have indicated earlier, happens frequently with Graham Greene and Faulkner.) The result would be that we finally say to ourselves: "All right! This is how it all seemed to one highly subjective, introspective and personally involved spectator. But it is not at all necessarily the way it really was." This does not in the least detract from our pleasure; but it is, surely, not exactly the sort of pleasure Joyce proposed to give us? In any case, if we do not recognise the precise nature of our pleasure a grave misinterpretation will result.

Joyce employed three devices to give us the illusion of detachment, of objectivity. (1) He built up a realistic background by the use of a meticulously accurate naturalistic detail. (2) He used this naturalistic realism to persuade us that he was quite detached intellectually from Stephen Dedalus. I refer to the frequent use of ironical comment on Stephen through sardonic contrasts. I will give examples presently. (3) He then boldly employed the subjective method to cast the spell of Stephen's personality over us, and he did it so well that it is with the greatest difficulty that we withhold from him an entirely uncritical sympathy. Almost any sequence in which Stephen Dedalus appears will show this triple device at work. Its main purpose is always the same: to lure us into the interior of Dedalus-Joyce; once we enter that magic cave the spell becomes well-nigh irresistible. Recall the opening page of *Ulysses*.

Mulligan emerges on the roof of the martello tower at Sandycove and does some fooling with the bowl of shaving-water. The whole picture is stereoscopically actual. On line twenty-six we read: "He peered sideways up and gave a long low whistle of call, then paused awhile in rapt attention, his even white teeth glistening here and there with gold points." Still pure naturalistic actuality. Then comes the single word: "Chrysostomos." We are inside Stephen's mind. The gold fillings in Mulligan's mouth have suggested to him the gold-mouthed orator, Dion Crysostomos. Actuality now returns, and the symphony of the interior stream is held off again until the third page; but not until—device number two—we have first been given a characteristic sub-ironic picture of Stephen with his poetic palm elegantly on his brow and his eyes self-pityingly on his ragged sleeve, symbol of his self-conscious poverty.

Then how the violins come up! "Pain that was not yet the pain of love fretted his heart. In sleep she came to him. . . ." A less cunning writer might have begun right away with that. This simple illustration of the triple device will suffice for the moment.

We note, however, that just as Mulligan literally presents his shaving-mirror to Stephen's eyes in these opening pages he is also, metaphorically, holding a mirror up to him for our benefit. Stephen sees himself through or in Mulligan's eyes. The whole saraband of characters who circle about Stephen do likewise. He (that is, he as the mask of Joyce) oscillates constantly between a cool observation of his fellows and a fevered contemplation of himself. This does not make him a Narcissus, but he is partially narcissistic in so far as he is incapable of seeing any character without relating him to himself.

Joyce's detachment, in short, is not only an illusion but, if we are deceived by it, a delusion. We might go so far as to call it a confidence trick which he plays on us. He was, also, no doubt playing it on himself. "See," he says to us and to himself, "how truthful I am about places, people, dates, details. How objective I am when I remove the mask from Cranly, Bloom, Lister, A.E., Father Conmee, Mulligan. See how I mock the dreams of this young fool Dedalus." We are deeply impressed. We applaud. We fail to notice that these characters only seem to go their own fair or unfair fleshly way – "seem", because all the time Stephen's life is lived at the centre, reflecting them, reflected in them, turning back constantly to himself from them, self-concerned, intellectual, an ego brooding on himself, *using* them, deploying them so as to see and express himself in his own private world which is, at every moment of self-consideration, not their world but his own private cosmos, the author's metaphysical subject. When this happens is Joyce "outside the thinker"? Are we? We, too, become part-Narcissus and the figures that shimmer in the pool under our eyes are, for those revealing moments, no longer objective. It is this Dedalus spell which is, in the ultimate, the spell of the *Portrait* and *Ulysses*. While we delight in it we must fear it. For what Joyce does is to blind us to the fact that this is, after all, an enclosed, private and highly personal world, the envelopment of his romantic *moi*, with which we identify ourselves. Joyce's world is not Dublin and all that. It is as private a world as that of Proust. But Joyce, too, is like Proust in search of essences which he reveals through what he calls epiphanies. If we were, then, to believe from Stephen's description of his aesthetic in *Stephen Hero* that Joyce was a classicist we would be very wide of the mark. The amount of romanticism infused into his work by his near-Narcissism and exhibitionism is abundant and pervasive. Does it matter? It matters enormously. For what we are dealing with is a man's life-sense, his view of life, his personal *manière de voir*.

I have earlier given my definition of a novel, when dealing with Faulkner, and must here repeat it with reference to Joyce's supposed objectivity. A novel is a prose-narrative dealing with a number of characters whom the author succeeds in making interesting and persuasive, and whom he deploys in a manner that, within his view of life, he considers fitting, and we with him. The external interest of his characters is primary in point of technique; their internal interest is primary in point of importance. They are decoys, no more. We do not read about them primarily for their sake; we read about them for what the author conveys by speaking in terms of character as a painter speaks in terms of colour and form. The crucial matter is the fittingness of the behaviour and fate of these characters. In a novel fitness is all.

This idea or notion of fitness is purely personal to the writer if he is an individual writer, and all good modern writing has, perforce, to be individual: i.e. it does not any longer present traditional or social ideas of what is fitting. But how can we speak of fitness unless we know what sort of spectacles the writer wears? This is more or less what Mlle Magny means when she says in *Les Sandales d'Empédocle* that all criticism is a form of autobiography: the reader walking arm in arm with the writer and saying, Yes, or No, in terms of his own experience, modifying it, enlarging it with the help of the author's spectacles. It is therefore essential to be aware of the constituents of Joyce's, or any writer's, way of looking at life.

I am aware that those who divide art from life will not be inclined to agree. To them art is self-contained. It is a picture hung on a wall about which we can be cognisant without any exterior assistance: an unmediated impact. I can only say that I do not agree, as I do not agree that I can look out of my study window without bringing to bear on the view before me a great deal of personal, traditional and acquired knowledge. To understand a work of art it is essential to grasp, as far as we can, the artist's *manière de voir*, and for this everything may be of use: knowledge of the artist's ambience, the influences that have worked on him, his place, his period, knowledge above all of the nature of the man himself. Over and over again, especially in reading the works of so self-centred a man as Joyce we must keep on adverting to the man.

What, then, are the outstanding *human* constituents of Joyce's subjectivity? The most striking thing in all his work is the impression he conveys of a nature torn between a painful sense of shame and an almost diabolical pride. The one postulates the other. If we glance over, say, the last hundred pages of *A Portrait of the Artist as a Young Man* we will note how often the two notes are struck in references to poverty. So, when Stephen talks to Davin in his room among the poor streets around Grantham Street, he is affected by the thought of the "starving Irish village" which is Davin's background. Leaving

Davin he is importuned by a flower-seller to whom he twice says: "I have no money." At the corner of Saint Stephen's Green this moment of "discouraged poverty" is prolonged in bitter hurt by the memory of the "tawdry tribute" paid to the patriot Wolfe Tone in 1898. The whole city, past and present, seems "venal" to him, a purchasable quantity. In a characteristic contrast he enters the College and begins to discuss the nature of the Beautiful with a priest, while the priest is lighting a fire with parsimoniously garnered candle-ends. "A desolating pity" begins "to fall on his easily embittered heart." (This may or may not be a symbol of the materials of which the fire of faith is made.) At the lecture which follows he does not even possess a sheet of paper on which to take notes, but immediately after it he reveals or boasts to some of his fellows that he has been to the office of arms to look up his family-tree. "I know you are poor," he says frankly to Lynch, and shares his last cigarette with him. When a fat student says he has joined a Field Club to help his botanical studies Stephen says dryly: "Bring us a few turnips and onions the next time you go out to make a stew." When, thinking of his love, he lies in bed writing a *villanelle* the contrasting squalor of his room is emphasised in the typical Joycean way: masochistic as for himself, sadistic as for his character. He is distracted by a louse crawling on his neck and "the life of his body, ill-clad, ill-fed, louse-eaten" makes him "close his eyelids in a sudden spasm of despair". Soon after, as he pauses outside Maples Hotel, its façade stings him "like a glance of polite disdain" and he imagines "the sleek lives of the patricians of Ireland housed in calm" and he derides the whole bat-like race of serfs, kowtowing to these nabobs, to whom he belongs. Cranly now joins him and he mocks, to him, his father's position and his own circumstances. "Born," Cranly says sardonically, "in the lap of luxury." It is in this passage of arms with Cranly, who is intent on bringing him to realise his condition and compromise with it, that he utters his final arrogant decision to serve nobody but to achieve his ambition to be whole and free.

That we should find a strain of bitter anger in Joyce's work is not surprising. He knows that his entire assets are his pride and his genius. His pride is boundless, and it is well that it should be, since a weaker man would have been wrecked by his circumstances. Granted this natural arrogance his circumstances will serve only to dilate his pride and strengthen it. He has the courage of his genius. His squalid surroundings become his slave instead of his master. He will rise through them, beyond them, sublimate them by his art so that the gush and whirr of the wings that surround him that day on the strand at Dollymount is less like the mechanical whirr of the wings of Dedalus than the whirring of the birds of inspiration about the head of the god Aengus which Meštrović used as a proposed model for the Irish coinage and which Yeats seized on as the symbol of poetry or genius.

Let us pause at this famous passage. It is illustrative of Joyce's oscillation between outer and inner. It also measures the quality of *his* "moments of vision", his epiphanies or showings-forth, his manifestations of the inner truth of reality, of what Terence Hewett in *The Voyage Out* called the "what's behind things".

We note the setting for the passage. It occurs at the end of Chapter IV which, we recall, opens with an account of Stephen's life after the famous Retreat. He has begun to order his life into a rosary of virtuous thoughts and acts; he has bound his hot flesh with the cincture of purity; he has submitted his mind to humility and piety. While he is in this mood a Jesuit, in a striking passage, toying with a loop of cord from the window-blind tries to lure him into the noose of the Order of Loyola. He returns to his home, described naturalistically, with the discarded crusts on the kitchen-table and the lees of tea in the bottoms of the jam-jars and jam-pots that do service for cups in this impoverished household. There he finds his brothers and sisters, in the fading afterglow of the dying day, sitting tranquilly about the table singing, in their young etiolated voices, that sad song of Tom Moore's, *Oft in the Stilly Night*. The scene is described in a naturalistic way, but it is probable that we are expected to hear Joyce's fine tenor voice lingering over the words (which he does not print) that give significance to the moment.

> *The smiles, the tears of boyhood years,*
> *The words of love then spoken . . .*

or, sardonically,

> *I feel like one who treads alone*
> *Some banquet hall deserted . . .*

At this point we have entered the young man's mind again. We next find him on the wide strand at Dollymount on a lovely day of "dappled seaborne clouds". The Jesuit's temptation has passed. (In all Joyce we will note that *Pilgrim's Progress* is reversed. Satan is tempted by Christ, but surmounts him.) Why, Stephen asks himself, has he not surrendered to the priest's pleadings? The answer is not stated but is clearly given in the following naturalistic description of a "squad" of "Christian Brothers" with "uncouth faces" tramping back to their monastery. We again oscillate inwards when the sight of them raises "a faint stain of personal shame and commiseration in his own" face. (In that Ireland to be a Christian Brother was to be on about the same low, intellectual level as a Plymouth Brother.) The clouds now dominate his mind, clouds blowing westward across the Irish Sea from Britain, from Europe, and they raise within him a confused music and old memories and names that gradually recede and merge into "a voice from beyond the world" calling him by his ancient name. Stephanos

Dedalos. Bous Stephanoumenos. Bous Stephaneforos. . . . It is here at last that the image of the flying artificer rises in his mind, dispelling those melancholy images of lost boyhood that Tom Moore's song had evoked the night before.

"His soul had risen out of the grave of boyhood, spurning her graveclothes. Yes. Yes. Yes. He would create proudly out of the freedom and power of his soul, as the great artificer whose name he bore, a living thing, new and soaring and beautiful, impalpable, imperishable."

Just then comes the epiphany to which all this has been leading. He sees, as in a vision, a true showing-forth, a girl standing among the rock-pools on long, white legs, her thighs as soft-hued as ivory, her bosom as soft and slight as a dark-plumaged dove. The image informs and enchants him. He cries out in joyful profanity. . . .

"Her image had passed into his soul for ever and no word had broken the holy silence of his ecstasy. Her eyes had called him and his soul had leaped at the call. To live, to err, to fall, to triumph, to recreate life out of life! A wild angel had appeared to him, the angel of mortal youth and beauty, an envoy from the fair courts of life, to throw open before him in an instant of ecstasy the gates of all the ways of error and glory."

We turn the page from that moment of release by revelation and we read: "He drained his third cup of watery tea to the dregs. . . ." The vision is mockingly and deliberately dispelled. But by this we have long ceased to as much as think about "who thinks", or whether James is outside Stephen or within him. The very device used to break the moment of vision reinforces it by pity.

I will give one other example of the Joyceian epiphany. It is the key that opens and closes the final and most revealing section of the novel. Stephen, late for an English lecture, imagines the crowded lecture-hall, and among the other students' skulls he imagines the skull of Cranly. It will be like the head of a priest appealing to the tabernacle for the other humble worshippers behind him. The following sentences then occur:

"Why was it that when he thought of Cranly he could never raise before his mind the entire image of his body but only the image of his head and face? Even now against the grey curtain of the morning he saw it before him like the phantom of a dream, the face of a severed head or death-mask, crowned on the brows by its stiff black upright hair as by an iron crown."

He goes on to elaborate a little his idea that Cranly is a fat priest, as it were a father-confessor, and then:

"Through this image he had a glimpse of a strange, dark cavern of speculation but at once turned away from it, feeling that it was not yet the hour to enter it. . . ."

The remaining part of the book leads us steadily towards this cavern which begins to open when Cranly and Stephen discuss religion and Stephen Diabolus rejects the last of his temptations, which, this time, revolves about Cranly's appeals to him to have pity on his mother. It is at the conclusion of this duel that Stephen makes his famous resolve to serve nothing in which he does not believe, home, fatherland or church, and to express himself "in some mode of life or art as freely as I can and as wholly as I can, using for myself the only arms I allow myself to use, silence, exile and cunning". Then, apparently quite casually, this prolonged and sinuous approach and conclusion is boiled down in his diary to one single image. He compares Cranly to Saint John the Baptist, the precursor of Christ (enemy of Stephen Diabolus) in these words:

"Also when thinking of him saw always a stern, severed head or death-mask as if outlined on a grey curtain or veronica. [We recall that grey curtain of the morning some eighty pages back.]

Decollation they call it in the fold. Puzzled for a moment by
Saint John at the Latin Gate. What do I see? A decollated precursor
trying to pick the lock."

"What do I see?" It is what Stephen Dedalus always sees:
not so much the actual person as the mirror in that person's
hand. What Stephen had seen at the entrance to his cavern of
speculation has been finally compressed into one image which
epiphanises the function of that one person in his life: Cranly
as the precursor picklock of his soul.

I think we must agree that these are not the sort of moments
of vision that illuminate life for Virginia Woolf. These are
moments infinitely expanded and fortified by Joyce's awareness
of the intellectual and moral content of all experience, giving
to his narrative a force and a meaning far beyond that of mere
aesthetic or sensory experience, radiating out of an intense
personal drama, which is also a metaphysical drama, in which
the antagonists bear many names and aspects – shame, pride,
surrender, revolt, good, evil, faith, unfaith, liberty, fraternisa-
tion – all of them so many elements in the interpretation of the
protean life-sense of one satanically and triumphantly arrogant
young Irishman bearing the banner with the device, *Non
Serviam*.

The point is that Joyce's epiphanies are, at their most effective,
far more than naturalistic summaries, far more than tinglings
along the nerves. They come from somewhere beyond the actual
of the there and the then, the external Dublin, the overt reality.
His mirror-bearers are men, but the images they reflect are
more than human, because they pierce into the young man's
depths where the struggle and the prize are both superhuman.
Recall the source of Mrs Woolf's phrase, "Moments of Vision".
It comes from Thomas Hardy's poem on

> *That mirror*
> *Which makes of men a transparency. . . .*

Who, he asks, hold it to us?

> That mirror
> Can test each mortal when unaware;
> Yea, that strange mirror
> May catch his last thoughts, whole life foul or fair,
> Glassing it—where?

Are Mrs Woolf's moments of vision intimation of things beyond the flaming ramparts of the world?

> All this was a long time ago, I remember,
> And I would do it again, but set down
> This set down
> This: were we led all that way for birth or death?

Which was the first Epiphany. Are we, in Joyce, led from one moment to another for birth or death? We will not rightly interpret his images if we think of them as merely illuminations on a psychological level.

If Joyce were merely a writer on that level he would not be the great literary hero of our time, have created a character that has caught the sympathy and imagination of the world. Dedalus is the *persona* or mask of a man who has handed back his ticket to the Almighty out of much more than human pity for the sufferings of humanity. He is a Promethean rebel defying Nature and God by the extent and intent of his rejection. He reinvokes Camus's statement about the individualist—that he must reject reality in order to affirm his own existence. "He wanted," we are told of Dedalus, "to meet in the real world the unsubstantial image which his soul constantly beheld." Not finding it there he will fly away like his fabulous namesake from and beyond the world. For his flight from Dublin is only the symbol of a far greater flight, and Dublin is his microcosm of a total divergence between man and God. In rejecting his native city and all it stood for he rejected his one fated field of life wherein he might have read the signatures of mortal things and made them tolerable, intelligible, meaningful. In their place he hoped to create, like a god, a new materiality. That splendidly blasphemous intent is to be found in his first novel wherein he makes the absurd claim for himself, as an artist, which his whole work in fact belies—that the artist *can* be detached. "The personality of the artist . . . refines itself out of existence, impersonalises itself, so to speak. The aesthetic image in the dramatic form is life purified in and reprojected from the human imagination." So far we can go with him. But then: "The mystery of aesthetic like that of material creation is accomplished. The artist, like the God of the creation, remains within or behind or beyond or above his handiwork, invisible, refined out of existence, indifferent, paring his fingernails. . . ."

So far one cannot go with him, since the artist cannot but be, himself, as much involved in the act of Creation as a man who makes bodily love to a woman and is reproduced in their child. To deny this is the ultimate revolt possible to man this side of suicide. The fascination of Joyce's denial is that he got away with it simply by recording the battle-cry in the *Portrait* and the progress of the battle in *Ulysses*; and sometimes one feels that *Ulysses* also records the defeat, but if it does so it records it so magnificently that the very record is yet another triumph. One must, however, utter a caveat. Joyce got away with it because he was Joyce. Nobody can imitate an autobiography. His books are unique and inimitable.

And though he got away with it he paid a dear price. There were certain limitations which no *Non Serviam* could overcome. He could record a revolt but he could never go farther than the revolt. There could be no sequel to those first two books. He had, by his too total rejection, walked himself into an impasse. That impasse was that he rejected intellectually everything in which he was involved emotionally, like a man who rejects in his brain a woman he loves in his deepest being. He was too involved in his own embryo ever really to be free of it. His past haunts him like a succubus. He can talk of nothing else. The flight and the chase are unending, so that his work has no ending except the recurrent denial, the recurrent flight, the smashing of the chandelier to the old strangled cry of, "With me all or not at all. *Non Serviam . . . Nothung!*", and Time's livid final flame leaps up and the ruin of all space; or the ending is two old washerwomen by the Liffey falling into night and sleep. In the splendid effort to cast away everything old and to create something utterly new he left himself with only one thing to write of, himself, child of Adam. Refusing to come to terms with the created world—which for him meant home, fatherland and church—he had no mechanism wherewith to come to terms with his own disconnected being. It is why all his characters have only one function—to be his mirror-bearers.

It was from the viewpoint of literature a magnificent revolt, and one would not wish that it did not happen, since the books won from it are so moving, so true and so revealing, not to mention so entertaining and so amusing. One cannot even wish that it had been less agonising, that he had not had to suffer the meanness of Edwardian Dublin, the stupidities of the Irish Church, the puritanism of its priests, the total intellectual poverty of his teachers, the misery of his own poor home, the bitter loneliness of his ravaged youth in that little, remote, untutored, inexperienced, conquered, timid and emotionally besotted island on the rim of the world. For out of it all he got, at least, something worth struggling with, a pressure to which he had to respond or die, something terrible enough to be worth denying. In denying it he clarified himself. Before he finished with Ireland he at least knew what he did not believe in, and had inklings of what was worthy of a man.

As I copy out these pages I find Mr J. B. Priestley asking,

challengingly, what influence Joyce really had, and by way of a
test asking if anybody could name twenty writers who show it.
But, surely, the rebellious anti-hero who is all over modern
fiction must have been enormously encouraged to parade
himself by the image of the arrogant revolt of Stephen Dedalus ?
The Twenties were ripe for just such a leader. He was their
bell-wether. All those young men and women who were
unhappy at school, who had had unkind or un-understanding
fathers, had mother complexes, hated the society in which they
grew, rebelled against convention, found themselves out on a
limb, conspired against their elders, rejected tradition, who saw
themselves, as Julien Sorel saw himself, forced to become
disciples of Tartuffe and Napoleon, all those hyper-sensitive
"sad young men"–who have become such a bore to us in the
long run, largely because so few of them had the intelligence
of Dedalus–were largely inspired by Joyce. Not that Joyce
invented the type or the idea. But he did resurrect in modern
terms an appealing type. The anti-hero goes back at least to
Don Quixote; he has gone on reappearing in many guises: to
think of a few at random, as Raskolnikov, Julien Sorel, Fréderic
Moreau, almost any of Hemingway's lone wolves, de Rastignac,
Adolphe, the son of *Father and Son*; he is the basis of *Les Faux-
Monnayeurs*; he turns up in Duhamel, Romain Rolland,
Marcel Aymé; Waugh poked fun at or through him, Greene
introduced him to God; he is any of Miss Bowen's doomed
heroines; he is all over Moravia's work; in Bloch, and Musil
and Svevo. But the list is endless. He will probably always be
with us now, or as long as youth believes in individual sincerity
and Ibsen's damned compact majority seems to betray it. The
only territories now left for him to conquer are those of the
cowboy and the Private Eye.